Dior

FINE JEWELLERY

Slipcase front: Detail of an advertisement for Miss Dior perfume, illustrated
by René Gruau. Photo © SARL René Gruau/www.renegruau.com.
Slipcase back: *Dovima with elephants, evening dress by Dior, Cirque d'Hiver,
Paris, August 1955*. Photo © The Richard Avedon Foundation.
© 2012 Assouline Publishing
601 West 26th Street, 18th floor
New York, NY 10001, USA
Tel.: 212-989-6810   Fax: 212-647-0005
www.assouline.com
Color separation by Luc Alexis Chasleries.
Text translated from the French by Denise Raab Jacobs.
Captions written by Laëtitia Dermoncourt.
Printed in China.
ISBN: 9781614280293

Jérôme Hanover

Dior

FINE JEWELLERY

ASSOULINE

“ Real jewellery is the highest point of great luxury. ”

Christian Dior,
The Little Dictionary of Fashion, Cassell & Co. Ltd.

1998, Place Vendôme, Paris

high jewelry is a respectable grande dame. She will not be pushed about. She lives by certain rules and principles, according to established codes and canons. She is esoteric, off-limits to the uninitiated; she keeps count in carats, measures fine metal in thousandths; she classifies her diamonds with letters and cabalistic ciphers in order to appraise them dispassionately, without emotion or poetry.[1] As the 1990s came to a close, high jewelry pieces were still created according to tradition: big rocks and little creativity, or to put it more elegantly, very prominently set stones. But not just any stones. The ancien régime still reigns over the Place Vendôme, where class inequality remains entrenched: On one side, the noblesse, represented by the four main precious stones—diamonds, rubies, emeralds, and sapphires; on the other, the more common, disparate, and unpronounceable stones. (We will return to this subject later.) The art of high jewelry is ageless; yet while its techniques have evolved, maturity is not modernity. At the close of the twentieth century, the world of high jewelry was ready for a change. What would it be?

Perhaps a little fantasy, but that would be like asking the moon to shine like the sun (or vice versa). High jewelry is fine jewelry, and fantasy can only belong to costume jewelry, which is, by definition, fake. Big rocks are serious business. The jewelers of the Place Vendôme, fearful of making a wrong move, and caught in a web of constraint and contradiction, chose to do nothing. The solution had to come from an outsider, an enfant terrible. To kill the father, a stranger had to penetrate the seraglio. In 1998 the house of Christian Dior launched its new high jewelry division; Victoire de Castellane was named creative director. "Is it a revolt?" "No, sire, it's a revolution."

> **Each creation tells its own extraordinary story, building on each other from one collection to the next.**

The high-end jewelers were perplexed, skeptical, and somewhat disdainful. One cannot confuse Place Vendôme with Avenue Montaigne. The former is the home of luxurious gems, the latter of luxurious fabrics.[2] Everything separates these two worlds: hard goods versus soft, durability versus seasonality, legacy and investment versus extravagant frivolity. Beyond the confusion of genres, the real surprise was the woman in charge. Typically, a jeweler was a man who remained in the shadows; suddenly, a woman stepped into the spotlight, a woman with the extraordinary name of Victoire. The great-granddaughter of Sylvia Hennessy, the great-niece of the dandy Boni de Castellane,[3] a descendant of Provençal counts, Victoire can trace her lineage back to the eleventh century. Victoire de Castellane is the consummate Parisienne, ultrafeminine, eccentric, and a fixture of the club scene at the Palace,[4] with her trademark bangs, dresses, and high heels.

And there was fantasy. In this new symphonic orchestra, the traditional quartet of precious gems played a more discreet part next to the chromatic richness of colored stones. In large or small scale, the pieces established a novel form of uninhibited jewelry. A new, dreamlike era was at hand, poetic and wondrous—a fantasy world.

1999, Avenue Montaigne, Paris

Victoire de Castellane introduced the first collection of high jewelry for Christian Dior. "Are you familiar with morganite, a sheer pink colored stone," wondered the press, "or iolite, with its unique shade of blue? The aristocratic transparency of chrysoberyl gemstones, the deeper hue of rhodolite garnets, or the delicate baby pink shade of kunzite? And, the finest of all, the 'padparadsha' [sic] sapphire, whose indescribable color oscillates between red and orange?"[5]

Of course, diamonds and other precious stones were still featured: A Diorissimo necklace, with small bells made of pearls and pavé-set emerald leaves, formed a spray of lily of the valley, one of the emblems of the couture house. Behind the facade of the deep-rooted traditions of high jewelry, the very foundation of a conservative profession was about to undergo a momentous change. Collections were given new, often primitive, names that evoked poetry and infinite nuances: The entire color range of geology was brought to the forefront. A rainbow of colored gemstones, which until then had been disregarded by "serious" jewelers, brought an entirely new vocabulary to the industry lexicon. The exotic-sounding names were as appealing to the ear as they were to the eye. The stones became fanciful characters in tales recounted by the pieces.

66 In this new symphonic orchestra, the traditional quartet of precious gems played a more discreet part next to the chromatic richness of colored stones. 99

High jewelry was once again a narrative. "Once upon a time, a vampire fell in love" was the inspiration for the Morsure (Bite) necklace[6] of dark red pear-shaped spinel stones that resemble blood droplets pearling at the jugular. "Once upon a time there was a reckless ladybug" who became the subject of the Carnivora Devorus ring:[7] A lacquered gold insect, attracted by a flower's diamond pistils, is about to be caught in a mechanical flytrap as the petals snap shut. "Once upon a time, fauna and flora lived in perfect harmony," as seen in the Idylle à Moyobamba bracelet:[8] A monkey, made of chiseled silver with a patina finish, is draped around a rose made of pink shell. "Once upon a time, she said 'Yes,'" and the word Oui on the eponymous ring[9] is spelled out with a diamond dotting the "i." Each creation tells its own extraordinary story, building on each other from one collection to the next, like an extended metaphor from text to text.

a s Victoire de Castellane set about creating the brand-new high jewelry division of Dior, she simply "pretended it had always existed."[10] In fact, Dior had included jewelry in his line as far back as 1947. It was an integral part of Corolle (Fall-Winter 1947), his second collection: "Diamond necklaces, [...] opulently designed necklaces with pear-shaped pearls."[11] Within a few months, Christian Dior had imposed his view on women's fashion: Couture came first, with his revolutionary New Look; then perfume, as an entire generation of women adopted Miss Dior as their fragrance; and finally, jewelry completed the wardrobe and entirely new silhouette. Together, they defined the look of a Parisienne, the woman everyone wanted to be, back then and perhaps still today. The stones, of course, were made of paste, and the opulence referred to the design, not the material. Costume jewelry was called *bijoux couture* (couture jewelry) and was worn as essential fashion accessories. From that moment on, every Haute Couture collection would include many pieces of jewelry: "Since we view costume jewelry as strictly decorative, its significant presence is important";[12] for example, "several brooches worn in new ways, and large hanging earrings";[13] "classic pearl necklaces were often replaced by strands of colored stones, especially coral, pale emeralds, and moonstones that have a springtime look";[14] "color is the main feature of jewelry; it illuminates the face";[15] "many large brooches, and lots of jet stones";[16] and "gardening tools, reproduced in rhinestone, executed with great finesse,"[17] "by their wit and charm, easily rival antique jewelry."[18]

In the fall of 1952, Christian Dior, whose fame had reached across the Atlantic (he even had a suite at the Plaza Hotel in New York City named for him), gave a series of interviews to *Woman's Illlustrated.* It was the gospel for Dior addicts in America, who latched onto the master's every word: "Jewellery is very important," he advised. "It may bring you the little touch of gaiety you need. Anyway, it always brings a certain sparkle to an outfit, which is most attractive. [...] Coloured stones and costume jewellery are excellent. Nothing is more elegant than a black sweater and skirt worn with a sparkling many-stoned necklace."[19]

Through his numerous collections, interviews, and notes, Christian Dior revealed his precise esthetic for jewelry. The fact that it was costume was of little importance. Couture jewelry made a statement. It was only a matter of choice, skill, and materials for the house of Dior to turn to high jewelry. And when the time was right, it was easy to see rhinestones become citrine or amethyst, morganite or aquamarine; as if by magic, all the stones became precious stones, and alchemy turned lead into gold. The color range, the size and scale, the sheer volume, the excess—all were already in place. Thus began, through the confluence of time and technology, an artistic dialogue between Christian Dior and Victoire de Castellane.

66 If Dior was the couturier of sumptuous galas, Victoire de Castellane has transcribed that same spirit and splendor into her jewelry collections. 99

and that discussion was animated! Searching the house of Dior's archives—"the identity of the company,"[20] as she calls them—Victoire de Castellane resurrected the designer. It seems that they share (or could have shared) a great deal. As if Dior had revealed his superstitions to her, Castellane reinterpreted them in her good-luck jewelry. As if he had spoken of his muse, Mitzah Bricard, and her affection for leopard prints, Castellane re-created the pattern in yellow gold and black enamel on a ring in the shape of an animal's paw.[21] He seemed to have shared the many horticultural secrets gathered from his Milly-la-Forêt garden, revelations that turned up in all of Castellane's collections, from the very first, in vegetable, floral, or whimsical form. The rose, the couturier's favorite flower, evoking his childhood and his parents' home above Granville in Normandy, is a recurring design. The rose has featured in every fashion show since 1947, in prints, embroidery, or brocade. The same applies to jewelry. Victoire de Castellane gathers roses in rustic bouquets,[22] designs rings with pavé roses of fancy diamonds in the same tone as the gold.[23] There are roses made of coral,[24] lacquered gold,[25] or small stones exquisitely framing a larger stone.[26] On the rare occasions when the rose is absent, the stem and thorns can be found forming a ring or hoop earrings.[27] Castellane references the man as well as his work: A part of Christian Dior himself exists in each of Victoire de Castellane's jewelry creations. She established her own galaxy within the Dior universe. Couture reigned supreme, and Castellane adopted and adapted all of its codes for her designs. For example, Castellane focused the same attention given to the lining of a garment on the finish of her Milly Carnivora rings: The lacquer reaches places that cannot be seen. She engraved a small star or moon under the stone of the Précieuse Rose rings that is only visible when the ring is removed. Another feature of couture applied to jewelry is the workmanship of a bow, set in pavé stones on a satin choker.[28] The references to couture even extend to the presentation of collections: At a press launch in 2005, pieces of jewelry appeared on a conveyor belt leading to a small podium, like models walking a runway.[29] Castellane calls her collections Tralala, Nougat, Diorette, Poulette—names that seem taken straight out of a Raymond Queneau text; and there are those that have the ring of faux Latin—Paradisea Cœur Secretus, Ancolia Veneinosa Pop, Reina Magnifica Sangria.[30] These appellations serve as explanations, brief textual analyses of her creations, and recall the heady days of Haute Couture when each dress had a name: Romance, May,

Concerto, Atout Cœur, Cocotte, or Cachottier, to mention just a few of Dior's designs. They share the same humor, which is both descriptive and coy, straightforward and offbeat. "We bring to jewelry design the essence of what we are: a Parisian couture house," affirms Sidney Toledano, Dior's CEO.[31] Hence the names, the use of color, the importance of a construction that enhances the material rather than the opposite.

“ Opals taste of anise, spinels of grenadine; tourmalines from Paraiba evoke menthol while those from Mali have the flavor of blueberries; cabochon emeralds resemble a Valda pastille; yellow beryls are reminiscent of mango confections; rubies are like cherries, and lacquered gold is a hard berlingot sugar candy. And diamonds are…a Schweppes! ”

From his very beginning as a couturier, Dior was inspired to design fanciful creations for the numerous balls held after the deprivations of World War II. "In the years following the war, the resurgence of society life took place in a flurry of parties and costumed balls. [...] These balls were the reason for the large number of evening gowns in [Dior's] collections, some so vertiginous that one wonders if the ball was the pretext for the dress or vice versa."[32] If Dior was the couturier of sumptuous galas, Victoire de Castellane has transcribed that same spirit and splendor into her jewelry collections. The gems have the velvet sheen of luxurious fabric.[33] Rose petals of sculpted rubellite, each stone set among rubies and spinels, bring to mind the luxury of embroidered silk taffeta; a lavender chalcedony set in a pavé fancy pink diamond ring seems to flutter like tulle—is it jewelry or embroidery? The ultimate synergy between haute couture and haute joaillerie has been achieved, as the collections echo each other, recounting the tales of the first in the language of the second.

My darling was naked, and knowing my heart well,
She was wearing only her sonorous jewels,
Whose opulent display made her look triumphant
Like Moorish concubines on their fortunate days.

When it dances and flings its lively, mocking sound,
This radiant world of metal and of gems
Transports me with delight; I passionately love
All things in which sound is mingled with light.

Charles Baudelaire, "Les Bijoux" ("The Jewels"), *Les Fleurs du Mal* (*Flowers of Evil*), 1857, translated by William Aggeler (Fresno: Academy Library Guild, 1954).

t he lascivious mistress who conquers the poet wears only jewelry, to emphasize her nudity. "I wanted to create Baudelairean jewelry,"[34] Castellane says. In other words, ornaments full of sensuality, as luminous objects of desire: "This...world of metal and...gems" is transformed from cold to "radiant." The minerals connect with the senses; erotic carats are luscious enough to eat: "Opals taste of anise, spinels of grenadine; tourmalines from Paraiba evoke menthol while those from Mali have the flavor of blueberries; cabochon emeralds resemble a Valda pastille; yellow beryls are reminiscent of mango confections; rubies are like cherries, and lacquered gold is a hard berlingot sugar candy.

> " Jewelry as candy—how ingenious!
> Or has the candy become jewelry? "

And diamonds are...a Schweppes!"[35] The overlapping color schemes confuse the senses of taste and sight, resulting in an appetite for stones. The colors of the Quatre Épices (Four Spices) brooch from Victoire de Castellane's first collection (1999) have an oriental flavor, establishing a more intimate relationship with gems. Jewelry has always been worn close to the body, against the skin; now, it will relinquish some of its formality and be even closer to the soul. Christian Dior had already used a similar sensory metaphor in 1947: "Jewels are [...] ear candy, daffodils, fumé blanc."[36]

Jewelry as candy—how ingenious! Or has the candy become jewelry? A tropism of regression? Not at all, just nostalgia for childhood—we like to play games at any age. The stones are appealing and addictive and can lead to excessive desire. A young girl's naive appreciation of such jewels will find its resolution in adulthood: If a three-carat stone could impress a five-year-old, it will take a sixty-carat stone to satisfy that same desire years later. The rings

> 66 A part of Christian Dior himself exists in each of Victoire de Castellane's jewelry creations. She established her own galaxy within the Dior universe. 99

from the Incroyables et Merveilleuses collection conjure an image of a young Victoire de Castellane "transported with delight" at the sight of the "opulent display" of fantastic jewels belonging to her grandmother, Sylvia Hennessy, and her best friend, Barbara Hutton. The jewels, like Proust's madeleine, unlock memory's door; unlike the madeleine, they are not dipped in tea, but appreciated visually. These reminiscences recall the pleasures of childhood, but do not exclude the consciousness of being grown-up (these jewels can cost millions of euros); they abolish the age of reason. The gemstones, so different in shape and size, are rendered similar by the warp of memory, and "simultaneously, like giants plunged into the years, they touch the distant epochs through which they have lived between, which so many days have come to range themselves—in Time."[37] The Incroyables et Merveilleuses collection—as most of Dior's gemstone pieces—symbolizes both girls as flowers and sensual women.

The new femininity, as esthetic as it was symbolic, was an iconoclastic catalyst in the typically masculine world of high jewelry. While women wear the jewels, the pieces were traditionally imagined, designed, made, sold, and bought by men. They speak more of power than of sensuality; even the semantics of jewelry reflect property rights and chauvinism. Dior jewelry, on the contrary, put women at the forefront of the discourse. The woman as alpha as well as omega; author and reader, creator and consumer; she is the center stone, majestically set; the independent woman has now become the client.

an iconoclast indeed, but also an iconologist. To fully understand Victoire de Castellane's rejection of classic-style jewelry, one needs to consider the period from the late nineteenth to the early twentieth century—a time when both jewelry and art history were revolutionized by the influence of Art Nouveau. Its organic and naturalist style impacted the esthetics of jewelry design. Think of René Lalique's disturbing bestiary, the imposing scale of his work, the discordant harmony of the stones he chose, his evil characters and utopian women, his use of enamel. The dreamlike universe he proposed was seductive to the intellectual elite but puzzling to the established bourgeoisie, fixed in its ways like a stone in its setting. Lalique had abolished the often tenuous and shifting boundaries that existed between art and jewelry design; understanding and accepting this new order required an open mind. The world of Dior high jewelry was a completely

66 Nothing is more elegant than a black sweater and skirt worn with a sparkling many-stoned necklace. 99

different place: Nature was domesticated, calmer; stories had happy endings; stones exploded with life and color; flowers never wilted; men were protective, and a vampire's bite was a promise of eternal love. It was the improbable meeting of a primitive Flemish painter and Walt Disney. A world of fantasy devoid of any danger, a fairy tale in which the princess has dressed up as a witch for her own amusement, to feel the thrill of scaring herself a little, but never really believing that she was anything other than a princess.

Beyond the stylistic connection to Lalique (the importance of color, the rediscovery of opals—a stone believed to contain evil powers ever since the Middle Ages—the specific uses of metal and gold, the esthetic of excess), it is through the more general relationship to creativity that one can reconcile these two approaches toward jewelry. Castellane's designs for Dior tend to eschew any imposed style; they answer only to their own desire. As an excellent example, look to the twenty pieces that form the Reines et Rois (Queens and Kings) collection: The ten rings are the queens, the ten pendants, the kings. These pieces are not simply twenty articles of high jewelry; they form a unique and indivisible work, an exercise of stylistic virtuosity. "The result is astonishing, because the kings and queens have the beauty of *gisants*, recumbent effigies. [...] The contrast between the opacity of the stones and the icy transparency of the diamonds is hypnotizing and noble. Even grave."[38] As is often the case, this Dior collection is a tribute to supreme craftsmanship. It represents the outstanding work of the finest Parisian ateliers at the service of a radical vision, an extreme esthetic, and authentic creativity. Indeed, this jewelry is art.

66 A rainbow of colored gemstones brought an entirely new vocabulary to the industry lexicon. 99

We have chosen a thematic rather than chronological approach to present Dior high jewelry: A simple linear perspective would not do justice to the stakes involved, the viewpoints, or even the esthetics. The collections do follow a certain order and build on each other: "I could not have designed Reines et Rois without having first designed La Fiancée du Vampire," says Victoire de Castellane, for reasons of technique as well as inspiration.[39] But together they form an entity that is incompartmentable, indivisible; more than a frieze, they depict a fresco: A tableau vivant in which pieces of jewelry move about like people, weaving a playful, sensual, and sensational tale. It is jewelry of contrast and paradox, of surprise and renewal, "controlled baroque,"[40] "veiled eroticism, explosively still, magically circumstantial."[41] Conventional jewelry design has been, until now, composed in alexandrine verse; for Dior, Victoire de Castellane has invented free verse.

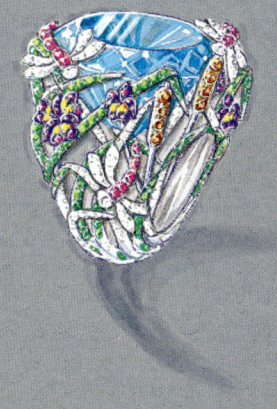

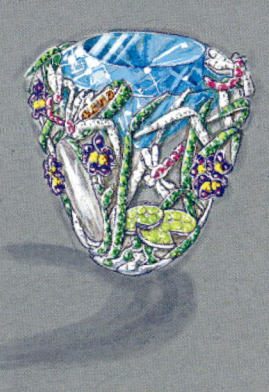

Victoire de Castellane

Notes

1. One carat is equivalent to 0.20 grams. The thousandth is the ratio of precious metal to alloy (for example, a piece of gold marked 750 contains 75% pure gold). The color grading scale for diamonds is alphabetical: D for the purest white, followed by E and so forth. (The scale begins at D rather than A to leave room for diamonds that might be even whiter than the D class.) A diamond of exceptional purity is designated IF (internally flawless), followed by an acronymic grading scale describing the impurities (VVS1 or 2 for very very slight inclusion, then VS1 and 2 for very slight inclusion, etc.).

2. Boucheron was the first jeweler to open a boutique in Place Vendôme in 1893. Cartier followed in 1898, Chaumet in 1902, and Van Cleef & Arpels in 1906. Place Vendôme became synonymous with French fine jewelry. Three subway stops away, Avenue Montaigne is the main axis of haute couture and luxury prêt-à-porter: Armani, Chanel, Christian Dior, Emanuel Ungaro, Jean-Louis Scherrer, Nina Ricci, and so on.

3. Boniface de Castellane was an esthete, a dandy, an avid collector, and a friend of Marcel Proust's. The character of Robert de Saint-Loup in *Remembrance of Things Past* was based on Boniface de Castellane.

4. From the late 1970s and through the 1980s, the Palace was the destination club for the jet set and the fashion world. Kenzo, Karl Lagerfeld, Claude Montana, Andy Warhol, Grace Jones, Prince, and Jean-Charles de Castelbajac were among its many regulars.

5. "Victoire de Castellane, le joyau de Dior" ("Victoire de Castellane, Dior's Jewel"), *Le Figaro Madame*, Claudine Hesse, April 24, 1999.

6. La Fiancée du Vampire collection, 2001.

7. Milly Carnivora collection, 2008.

8. Idylle aux Paradis collection, 2009.

9. Oui collection, 2005.

10. Victoire de Castellane, in an interview on April 21, 2011.

11. Press release for the Fall-Winter 1947 Corolle collection.

12. Press release for the Fall-Winter 1948 Ailée collection.

13. Press release for the Fall-Winter 1949 Milieu du Siècle collection.

14. Press release for the Spring-Summer 1953 Tulipe collection.

15. Press release for the Fall-Winter 1951 Longue collection.

16. Press release for the Fall-Winter 1950 Oblique collection.

17. Press release for the Spring-Summer 1952 Sinueuse collection.

18. Press release for the Fall-Winter 1952 Profilée collection.

19. "How to Dress the Dior Way," *Woman's Illustrated* no 932, October 11, 1952, highlighted by Christian Dior.

20. Victoire de Castellane, in an interview on April 21, 2011.

21. Mitza ring, 2003.

22. Diorette collection, 2006.

23. Bagatelle collection, 2000.

24. Gwendoline collection, 2000, and Rose Dior Pré Catelan collection, 2010.

25. Diorette collection, 2006.

26. Précieuse Rose collection, 2006.

27. Bois de Rose collection, 2010.

28. Ingénue Eugénie necklace from the Couture collection.

29. Presented to the press on October 9, 2005.

30. Belladone Island collection, 2007.

31. Interview on April 11, 2011.

32. Farid Chenoune, *Dior*, Assouline, 2007.

33. Le Bal des Roses collection, 2011.

34. Victoire de Castellane, in an interview on April 21, 2011.

35. Ibid.

36. Press release for the Corolle collection, Fall-Winter 1947.

37. Marcel Proust, *Time Regained*, translated by Andreas Mayer and Terence Kilmartin (New York: Modern Library, 2003).

38. "Dior Joaillerie a trouvé sa reine" ("Dior Jewelry Has Found Its Queen"), *Le Figaro*, Fabienne Reybaud, July 9, 2009.

39. Interview on April 21, 2011.

40. Ibid.

41. André Breton, *L'Amour Fou*.

Chronology

1947:   Christian Dior presents his first Haute Couture collection
and his first pieces of costume jewelry.

1998:   Victoire de Castellane is appointed creative director of Dior Jewelry.

1999:   Opening of the Dior Joaillerie boutique at 28 Avenue Montaigne in
Paris. Launch of the first fine jewelry collections: Milly-la-Forêt,
Couture, and Excentrique. Introduction of the first rings from
the Incroyables et Merveilleuses collection. Mitza collection.

2000:   Bagatelle and Gwendoline (Pré Catelan) collections.

2001:   Soumission collection and Mimioui rings.
Opening of the boutique at 8 Place Vendôme in Paris. Launch of
Fiancée du Vampire and Favorite du Harem collections.

2002:   Le Bal de la Fiancée du Vampire: A ball is held at the Ritz hotel
to celebrate the opening of the Dior Joaillerie boutique in
Place Vendôme.

2003:   Le Coffret de Victoire collection.

2004:   Gourmette de Dior collection.
Le Bestiaire Fantastique fine jewelry collection.

2005:   Launch of the Oui ring.

2006:   Diorette collection.
Les Précieuses collection.

2007:   Four pieces from the Belladone Island fine jewelry collection
are previewed on Secondlife.com.
Presentation of the Belladone Island collection in the Monet
Nymphéas gallery at the Orangerie Museum in Paris.
Launch of Petite Série Limitée Mimioui au Bal.

2008:   Dior Joaillerie participates in the Biennale des Antiquaires for the
first time, and introduces the Milly Carnivora collection.

2009:   Idylle aux Paradis and La Bague collections.
Reines et Rois collection.

2010:   Bois de Rose collection.
Rose Dior Pré Catelan collection. Dior Joaillerie participates
in the Biennale des Antiquaires for the second time.

2011:   Le Bal des Roses collection.

Victoire de Castellane

Dior

FINE JEWELLERY

The final gouache drawing. The creation of a piece of jewelry is a long process, which starts with a sketch by Victoire de Castellane on a Post-it note. After weeks of reflection and work with the studio comes the final gouache, a precise color drawing showing the piece from several angles. Here, the gouache drawing of a ring for the Incroyables et Merveilleuses collection. Photo © Christian Dior.

The Dior Jewelry shop windows. Since the creation of Dior Jewelry in 1999, Victoire de Castellane has wanted to offer the public creative, artistic, fairy-tale window displays. Here, a detail of the windows for the boutique at 8 Place Vendôme in Paris, representing the Dior mansion at 30 Avenue Montaigne in miniature. Photos © Sophie Carre.

Victoire de Castellane has been the creative director of Dior Jewelry since its inception in 1999. Photo © Patrick Demarchelier. Right: A wall in de Castellane's studio, covered in butterflies. Photo © Stéphane Muratet.

Victoire de Castellane's studio. The inspiration wall in de Castellane's studio on rue François 1er in Paris, covered in butterflies, photo cutouts, and cartoon characters, reflects the personality and boundless imagination of the designer. Photo © Stéphane Muratet.

French savoir faire. Like all Dior Jewelry creations, these two exceptional pieces have been made completely by hand in Parisian ateliers. Each stage of fabrication—sculpting the setting, cutting the stones, applying the lacquer—is a unique expression of French craftsmanship. Left: the Reina Magnifica Sangria necklace from the Belladone Island collection. Photo © Guido Mocafico. Right: the Bal de l'Opera necklace from Le Bal des Roses collection. Photo © Erwan Frotin.

The Dior Jewelry boutique at 8 Place Vendôme, opened in 2001, redesigned by American architect Peter Marino in 2010, is an homage to Monsieur Dior's taste for the grand French style of the 18th century. Here, the staircase and atrium. The address itself is a discreet reference to the superstitious couturier who particularly loved the number 8. Photos © Kristen Pelou.

Lucky lily of the valley. Lily of the valley was Christian Dior's favorite flower. On presentation days, he would have sprigs of it stitched into the lining or hem of his dresses. It also inspired the Muguet dress in the Haute Couture collection of Spring-Summer 1957, and the Diorissimo necklace set with emerald, diamonds, and pearls. Left: © Laziz Hamani. Right: © Thomas Hugues.

The taste for the 18th century. The Dior Jewelry advertising campaign of 2010, presenting the Bois de Rose and Rose Dior Bagatelle collections, was inspired by Christian Dior's love for the refinement of the grand 18th-century French style, such as elegant decorative moldings, marble chimneys, and gilt mirrors. Photos © Inez van Lamsweerde and Vinoodh Matadin/trunkarchive.com.

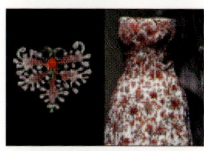

Floral inspiration. Flowers were always a great source of inspiration for Christian Dior, who loved gardens and all things botanical. Since its founding in 1999, Dior Jewelry has largely drawn its motifs from the world of flowers for its collections. Left: the Fleuro Poisonus Spinella ring in white gold, diamonds, yellow diamonds, pink sapphires, spinels, tsavorite and demantoid garnets, and lacquer, from the Belladone Island collection, inspired by carnivorous plants. Photo © Guido Mocafico. Right: © Laziz Hamani.

Belladone Island. In February 2007, at the Nymphéas de Monet gallery in the Orangerie museum, Dior Jewelry presented the Belladone Island collection. All the pieces carry exotic, imaginary plant names, such as the Dracula Spinella Devorus ring shown here, whose chalcedony petals open and close to reveal a large spinel surrounded by sapphires, diamonds, and white gold claws. Photos © Guido Mocafico.

Le Coffret de Victoire. Victoire de Castellane gathers stones and stories from the four corners of the earth to create unique pieces of unbridled creativity that collectors find impossible to resist. Right: Bollywood earrings in yellow gold, diamonds, green opals, yellow beryls, spessartite and tsavorite garnets, pink sapphires, Paraiba tourmalines, and lacquer. Photo © Anna Leroy. Left: still from the Bollywood film *Devdas*, directed by Sanjay Bhansali, 2002. Photo © Eros International/courtesy Everett Collection.

The Reines et Rois collection embodies the idea that jewelry is everlasting while human life is finite. This collection comprises 20 rings and pendants with a skull motif rendered in various stones, in settings of diamonds and platinum. Left: Roi de Quartznoir pendant in platinum, white gold, diamonds, and black rutilated quartz. Right: from left to right, top to bottom: Roi d'Opalie, Roi de Sugilie, Roi de Rutilie, Roi d'Obsidienne, Rois de Crocidolite and Roi de Charoïte pendants. Photos © Anna Leroy.

The couture label. Dior Jewelry pays homage to Dior Haute Couture with the Gourmette ring. As with the label sewn into the back of Dior garments, the ring displays what is ordinarily hidden: the logo, piece number, size, hallmark, and gold content. Left: Photo © Christian Dior. Right: © Laziz Hamani.

Costume balls and their characters. Christian Dior loved costume balls. Right: Daisy Fellowes, in a Dior gown, at the costume ball hosted by Charles de Beistegui in Venice in 1951. Photo © Cecil Beaton/Condé Nast Publications Ltd. Left: The large center stone of the Incroyables et Merveilleuses Lapin ring, in yellow gold, diamonds, amethyst, multicolored sapphires, emeralds, and black spinels, recalls this taste for extravagance. Photo © Anna Leroy.

Exceptional craftsmanship. It is a point of honor that each piece of Dior Jewelry is fabricated entirely by hand, by the finest French artisans, from the setting of each stone on the delicate Bois de Rose ring, to the lacquer on pieces such as the Idylle à Moyobamba bracelet, from the 2009 Idylles au Paradis collection. Left © Stéphane Muratet. Right © Vincent Dufeu.

Hidden jewels. Certain pieces in the Belladone Island and Milly Carnivora collections, inspired by carnivorous flowers, feature articulated miniature mechanisms that can open to reveal a secret element. Here, the chrysoprase petals of the Grani Opalia Devorus ring open to reveal a 9.47-carat opal, multicolored sapphires, tsavorite and spessartite garnets, amethysts, and white gold claws. Photos © Guido Mocafico.

Le Bestiaire Fantastique is a collection of rings, hand jewelry, necklaces, and earrings conceived around the opal, Victoire de Castellane's favorite stone. Left: the Medusa ring in white gold, diamonds, fire opals, black opals, multicolored sapphires, and Paraiba tourmaline. Photo © Nicolas Bluche. Right: Illustration by René Gruau, published in *Femina IV,* 1949. Photo © SARL René Gruau/www.renegruau.com.

Dior's vegetable garden. Christian Dior loved his vegetable gardens as much as his flower gardens, and his life revolved around them. Since 1999, Dior Jewelry has rendered green peas, turnips, cherries, and raspberries in precious stones and metals. Left: Drawing by Christian Dior for a menu, January 2, 1940. Photo © Christian Dior. Right: Earrings from Le Coffret de Victoire collection in yellow gold, diamonds, jade, pink sapphires, and lacquer. Photo © Anna Leroy.

The rose, another of Christian Dior's favorite flowers, symbolized the childhood he spent in the garden at his parents' house in Granville, in Basse-Normandie. Left, from top: Rose Dior Bagatelle ring in pink gold and pink diamonds; Bois de Rose ring in pink gold and pink diamonds. Photos, from top: © Studio 36, © Anna Leroy. Right: Marie-Antoinette's rose garden at Versailles. Photo © François Halard.

The famous Pré Catelan gardens in the Bois de Boulogne gave their name to a collection of rings featuring roses carved from coral, onyx, quartz, and chalcedony, another nod to Dior's favored flower. Left: René Gruau's sketch for a 1956 Diorissimo advertisement. Photo © SARL René Gruau/www.renegruau.com. Right: Rose Dior Pré Catelan ring, in yellow gold, diamonds, yellow sapphires, and black onyx, depicting a honeybee gathering pollen from two onyx roses. Photo © Christian Dior.

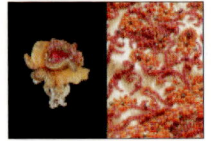

Le Bal des Roses collection calls to mind Christian Dior's magical ability to transform his beloved flowers into dresses for his couture collections and sumptuous gowns for the costume balls he so enjoyed. Left: the Bal Vénitien ring in yellow gold, diamonds, colored diamonds, pink spinel, fire opals, spessartite garnets, and pink sapphires. Photo © Erwan Frotin. Right: detail of beadwork on the bodice of the Corail gown, from the Spring-Summer 1959 collection. Photo © Laziz Hamani.

The garden at Milly-la-Forêt. Since the first collection in 1999, Victoire de Castellane has paid homage to Monsieur Dior's gardens at Milly-la-Forêt. Left: The Milly-la-Forêt necklace, in yellow gold, diamonds, emeralds, rubies, amethysts, chrysoprase, onyx, jade, cultured pearls, and coral, represents the garden where Dior loved to relax on weekends. Photo © Thomas Hugues. Right: Christian Dior in his garden at Milly-la-Forêt. Photo © 2011 Association Willy Maywald/Artists Rights Society (ARS), New York/ADAGP, Paris.

Diorette. Left: The Diorette ring, in yellow gold, diamond, amethyst, mandarin and tsavorite garnet, and lacquer, with its little ladybug, symbolizes the eternal freshness of a bouquet of wildflowers. Photo © Studio 36. Right: Christian Dior in his garden at Milly-la-Forêt. Photo © André Ostier.

Haute Couture jewelry. Le Bal des Roses collection expresses the union of nature with the refinement of the House of Dior couture, illustrating the connection between Christian Dior and high jewelry. The roses in this collection represent ladies dressed in sumptuous ball gowns. Left: Bal de Paris ring in white gold, diamonds, white quartz, and rubies. Photo © Erwan Frotin. Right: Red satin Concerto evening gown from the Fall-Winter 1957 collection. Photo: Collection Musée Christian Dior, Granville.

Milly Carnivora. In 2008, a family of eight new varieties of carnivorous flowers, the Milly Carnivora collection, was introduced to the Dior Jewelry garden. Right: The Carnivora Devorus pendant, in yellow gold, diamonds, tsavorite garnets, multicolored sapphires, Paraiba tourmalines, and lacquer on a silken cord, opens to reveal a gold and lacquer ladybug. Photo © Anna Leroy. Left: Detail of Christian Dior's La Flûte Enchantée gown, 1950. Photo © Sacha Van Dorssen.

Mitzah Bricard, Christian Dior's muse, friend, and close adviser, was particulary fond of leopard print. Right: the Mitza ring, in yellow gold and black lacquer, pays homage to Madame Bricard. Photo © Christian Dior. Left: detail of a 1949 advertisement for Miss Dior perfume, illustrated by René Gruau. Photo © SARL René Gruau/www.renegruau.com.

Victoire de Castellane's gouache drawing for the Bal de Mai necklace from Le Bal des Roses collection. Photo © Christian Dior.

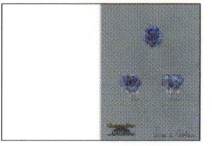

Victoire de Castellane's gouache drawing for the Bal Bleu Nuit ring from Le Bal des Roses collection. Photo © Christian Dior.

Acknowledgments

The publisher wishes to thank the Maison Dior for its help in the publication of this book.

Thanks also to: Gail de Courcy-Ireland; Alexandra Kadlec, Artists Rights Society; Leigh Montville and Aaron Seigal, Condé Nast Publications; Laziz Hamani; Nigel Boekee; Michele Filomeno; Sylvie Nissen, SARL René Gruau; and Justin Rose, Trunk Archive.

...ase front: Detail of an advertisement for Miss Dior perfume, illustrated
...ené Gruau. Photo © SARL René Gruau/www.renegruau.com.
...se back: *Dovima with elephants, evening dress by Dior, Cirque d'Hiver,
...August 1955*. Photo © The Richard Avedon Foundation.
...ing pages: Christian Bérard's sketch of the Bar suit, 1947.
...tion Musée Christian Dior, Granville. © 2011 Artists
...Society (ARS), New York/ADAGP, Paris.
...2 Assouline Publishing
...st 26th Street, 18th floor
...rk, NY 10001, USA
...2-989-6810   Fax: 212-647-0005
...ssouline.com
...aration by Luc Alexis Chasleries.
...nslated from the French by Gail de Courcy-Ireland.
...n China.
...81614280279

Dior

Slip...
by R...
Slip...
Paris...
Follo...
Colle...
Right...
© 201...
601 W...
New Yo...
Tel.: 21...
www.a...
Color se...
Text tra...
Printed...
ISBN: 97...

Caroline Bongrand

Dior

ASSOULINE

Bérard

Introduction

On February 12, 1947, Christian Dior transformed the international codes of elegance with his very first collection. He was forty-two years old. As he set out on this new phase of his life, Dior was unaware that a very special destiny awaited him: He would know extraordinary success, instant fame beyond all borders, and imprint his inimitable style on the world, made of dreams and enchantment. In a matter of years, Dior came to symbolize the utmost in luxury, elegance, and excellence. He offered women a personal vision of happiness and beauty that went far beyond fashion, savoring and reinventing a sophisticated lifestyle whose roots lie in European history and Parisian style. On this great heritage he built the House of Dior, making it the ultimate icon of luxury. Today this heritage lives on in the audacious talents of his successors, who nurture a close creative bond with the legacy of Monsieur Dior.

When Dior founded his couture house in December 1946, he had already lived several lives: He had enjoyed a happy, secure childhood in Granville, a bohemian lifestyle in Paris between the wars, and a spell as a talented, well-respected director of an art gallery. His family had experienced personal loss and financial ruin. He had apprenticed as a designer, lived through the painful years of World War II, and only when he was thirty did he discover couture, or rediscover his love of drawing. In a world still reeling from the horrors of war, Dior wanted to free women from an atmosphere tainted by strict rationing and limits on textile purchases. His true desire was to give women back their beauty and femininity. The man who had created fancy-dress costumes for his friends in Granville as a child wanted the couturier to become the magician in fairy tales. He worked tirelessly, literally conducting his seamstresses with a bamboo rod to make gorgeous dresses that seemed to come straight out of a fairy tale by Perrault, whose stories were among his childhood favorites. He dreamed of filling the world with *femmes fleurs*, his "flower women."

The Beginning

ior's love of flowers dates back to his childhood in Granville, on the Normandy coast. The son of Maurice and Madeleine Dior, Christian came from an affluent, upper-class family. They lived in a pink house surrounded by gray gravel, perched on the edge of a cliff. Five generations of the Dior family had established a profitable business, passed down from father to son, dealing in agricultural fertilizers. In the 1920s the company adopted the advertising slogan "Dior, c'est de l'or"—Dior is pure gold. The house overlooked the sea, but more importantly,

Dior

Slipcase front: Detail of an advertisement for Miss Dior perfume, illustrated
by René Gruau. Photo © SARL René Gruau/www.renegruau.com.
Slipcase back: *Dovima with elephants, evening dress by Dior, Cirque d'Hiver,
Paris, August 1955*. Photo © The Richard Avedon Foundation.
Following pages: Christian Bérard's sketch of the Bar suit, 1947.
Collection Musée Christian Dior, Granville. © 2011 Artists
Rights Society (ARS), New York/ADAGP, Paris.
© 2012 Assouline Publishing
601 West 26th Street, 18th floor
New York, NY 10001, USA
Tel.: 212-989-6810   Fax: 212-647-0005
www.assouline.com
Color separation by Luc Alexis Chasleries.
Text translated from the French by Gail de Courcy-Ireland.
Printed in China.
ISBN: 9781614280279

Dior

Caroline Bongrand

ASSOULINE

Bérard

Introduction

On February 12, 1947, Christian Dior transformed the international codes of elegance with his very first collection. He was forty-two years old. As he set out on this new phase of his life, Dior was unaware that a very special destiny awaited him: He would know extraordinary success, instant fame beyond all borders, and imprint his inimitable style on the world, made of dreams and enchantment. In a matter of years, Dior came to symbolize the utmost in luxury, elegance, and excellence. He offered women a personal vision of happiness and beauty that went far beyond fashion, savoring and reinventing a sophisticated lifestyle whose roots lie in European history and Parisian style. On this great heritage he built the House of Dior, making it the ultimate icon of luxury. Today this heritage lives on in the audacious talents of his successors, who nurture a close creative bond with the legacy of Monsieur Dior.

When Dior founded his couture house in December 1946, he had already lived several lives: He had enjoyed a happy, secure childhood in Granville, a bohemian lifestyle in Paris between the wars, and a spell as a talented, well-respected director of an art gallery. His family had experienced personal loss and financial ruin. He had apprenticed as a designer, lived through the painful years of World War II, and only when he was thirty did he discover couture, or rediscover his love of drawing. In a world still reeling from the horrors of war, Dior wanted to free women from an atmosphere tainted by strict rationing and limits on textile purchases. His true desire was to give women back their beauty and femininity. The man who had created fancy-dress costumes for his friends in Granville as a child wanted the couturier to become the magician in fairy tales. He worked tirelessly, literally conducting his seamstresses with a bamboo rod to make gorgeous dresses that seemed to come straight out of a fairy tale by Perrault, whose stories were among his childhood favorites. He dreamed of filling the world with *femmes fleurs*, his "flower women."

The Beginning

dior's love of flowers dates back to his childhood in Granville, on the Normandy coast. The son of Maurice and Madeleine Dior, Christian came from an affluent, upper-class family. They lived in a pink house surrounded by gray gravel, perched on the edge of a cliff. Five generations of the Dior family had established a profitable business, passed down from father to son, dealing in agricultural fertilizers. In the 1920s the company adopted the advertising slogan "Dior, c'est de l'or"—Dior is pure gold. The house overlooked the sea, but more importantly, it was the setting for Madeleine Dior's magnificent garden. Madeleine was an elegant lady who loved to entertain and enjoyed tending her seaside garden. Christian, the second of five children, would follow her around it in wonder, sharing her passion for the trees and flowers. As a teenager, he sketched its fountains, furniture, and flowers, which he cared for passionately; to this day, seasoned landscape designers praise the bold creativity of the garden in which he grew up. As a child, Dior would pore over the seed catalogs of the Maison Vilmorin-Andrieux, memorizing the names and descriptions of the flowers. It was the Belle Époque, a carefree time when laughter often tinkled out from the winter garden, which had been custom built for Madeleine, and an Oriental influence ran throughout the house, courtesy of Hokusai. Madeleine Dior liked to shop for clothes in Paris, on Rue Royale, invariably taking young Christian with her. In truth, he was her favorite, for he shared her love of horticulture, good taste, and elegance.

In 1910, the family moved to Paris, keeping the Granville house as their vacation home. Christian discovered the Passy neighborhood and the fashionable interior design of the time, inspired by eighteenth-century French court style. He would forever associate that style with those happy years and sought to re-create the atmosphere he called "neo–Louis XVI" in his couture house. "White wood paneling, white lacquer furniture, gray draperies, French doors with beveled glass, bronze wall lamps with small shades." Sober, simple, classic, and Parisian.

Young Christian was passionate about literature, music, painting, and Art Nouveau. He and his friends attended every reception and gallery opening. Dior already appreciated and admired Renoir, Toulouse-Lautrec, and Vuillard; now he discovered Matisse, Picasso, Braque, Stravinsky, and Schoenberg. From the Ballets Russes to German expressionist cinema, Dior embraced his times. He dreamed of being an architect. When he announced to his parents that he wanted to attend the Fine Arts School in Paris after graduating with his baccalaureate, they categorically refused: no bohemian lifestyle for their son! His mother wanted him to be a diplomat. He attended the Political Studies Institute in Paris, but soon learned that his heart was elsewhere. It was the Roaring Twenties and Le Bœuf sur le Toit, the bar-restaurant founded by Louis Moysès, was the epicenter of Parisian avant-garde artistic life in the period between the wars. This was when Christian met the people who would become his lifelong friends. Through Jean Cocteau and Max Jacob he mingled with the brightest intellectuals and artists of his generation. He struck up a friendship with the painter Christian Bérard, who knew how to transform the mundane "into an intense, nostalgic, fairy-tale world." Dior bought as many of Bérard's works as he could, covering his bedroom walls with the artist's paintings. He also met the composer Henri Sauguet and the fashion illustrator Jean Ozenne, both of whom would have a decisive influence on his future. Together they exchanged ideas, played music, and pondered the ups and downs of existence at Le Bœuf sur le Toit: "Amazing gatherings where we eagerly savored our friendship."

At the age of twenty-two, Christian Dior chose his first career: director of an art gallery. Dior's parents initially refused to help, but in the end they funded his business venture, on one condition—the Dior name could not appear on the door. In 1928 Dior went into business with Jacques Bonjean, a former army acquaintance of his brother Raymond, and opened a gallery named the Galerie Jacques Bonjean. "Our plan was to show the works of the artists we respected most, Picasso, Braque, Matisse, and Dufy, alongside painters we knew personally and admired, Christian Bérard, Salvador Dalí, Max Jacob, the Berman brothers." The gallery presented major theme shows with international appeal. In 1931, *Peintres allemands contemporains* [Contemporary German Painters] featured works by Klee, Ernst, and Otto Dix; it was followed in 1932 by *L'Époque héroïque du Cubisme* [The Heroic Age of Cubism]. That year, Dior befriended Leonor Fini and was the first to show her works in France. Meanwhile, at a Max Jacob exhibition, he met a young poet by the name of Pierre Colle.

Dior had a keen eye for art. He loved artists, and considered them as brothers in arms. He became a skilled dealer in modern art, and his talent was spotted by Gertrude Stein, who became a trusted client. Christian Dior was a happy man.

The Wall Street crash of 1929 pitched America into the Great Depression, which spread to France within a year. In 1930, Christian Dior learned that one of his brothers had an incurable disease. Devastated by the news, Madeleine Dior died of heartache. "Tragedy had come into our happy and secure family." Soon after, Maurice Dior's business and personal investments collapsed. By 1931 he was completely ruined. The family was reduced to selling off its furniture, paintings, and art.

In the harsh economic climate of 1932, the Bonjean gallery was forced to close down, and Bonjean declared bankruptcy. "I was out on my own and soon learned what life was really about," Christian Dior would later say. When he could no longer afford his own apartment, his friends offered to take him in.

Dior joined Pierre Colle's gallery, but it too was hit by the crisis: "We went from financial losses to bailiffs calling while we were still mounting exhibitions of surrealist and abstract painting." The gallery featured works by Dalí, Calder, Giacometti, Picasso, Derain. The *Surrealism* exhibition, held in 1933, included works by Dalí, Ernst, Klee, Breton, Giacometti, and Miró, and was widely praised by the critics, with the avant-garde featuring alongside recognized talent. The gallery also organized retrospective exhibitions, notably for Max Jacob, Utrillo, Braque, and Marcoussis. This artistic adventure continued until 1934, when the gallery was forced to close, another victim steamrollered by the crisis. The owner of Le Bœuf sur le Toit, "generous Moysès," as Dior liked to call him, still welcomed his loyal clients who were now down on their luck and even housed Dior for free in the attic room above the restaurant, where everything leaked—the roof and the water pipes—but "with the help of a few bottles [of wine], a piano, and a phonograph, we chased our cares away by inventing crazy stories."

Christian Dior had lost everything that had formed his childhood: his mother, his family roots, and the comfort that had given him a certain carefree existence. There was nothing left: The Paris apartment and the Granville house were gone. "After all the skipped meals and anxiety, I fell gravely ill."

His friends pooled together to send him to the Balearic Islands to rest for a year. "Getting away from Paris, where the artistic activity of others had sufficed to keep me happy, I discovered a profound and new desire to create something of my own." He studied the techniques of tapestry, which fascinated him as an art, and began creating tapestry cartoons. Thrilled with this novel pursuit, he considered opening a workshop, but soon realized he could not drum up enough interest to sustain it. His love of drawing had been revived, however; his destiny was taking shape.

Back in Paris, Dior reconnected with his father and sister and convinced them to move to the South of France. He remained in Paris, scouring employment ads, hoping to find a job. After being denied an administrative post in the house of couturier Lucien Lelong, he exclaimed: "I think I would be much better at couture." He wasn't wrong. Luckily, a painting he had entrusted to an American dealer was sold in the United States, and the family could breathe a little more easily.

Jean Ozenne, a fashion illustrator and friend of Christian's, invited him to stay in his apartment on Quai Henri-IV. "After watching him work while I sat there twiddling my thumbs, I decided to imitate him." He worked alongside Max Kenna, another friend of Ozenne's and also a fashion sketch artist, who taught Dior how to use a paintbrush and utilize colors. Ozenne encouraged Dior, offering to show his sketches when he pitched to potential clients. Christian agreed, as long as his name would not appear on any drawings. One night, Ozenne came home victorious: He had sold six of Dior's drawings. "I was amazed. Those 120 francs, the result of a close and caring friendship, was like the first ray of sunlight after a long night; it would change my future, and still shines bright in my life today." Christian Dior became an illustrator for the women's page in *Le Figaro*, at a time when he met and became friends with René Gruau, one of the most famous illustrators of the day. Years later, when Dior established his own couture house, he asked Gruau to create images for Dior perfumes that would become legends in themselves.

Christian Dior built his reputation sketch by sketch. A friend introduced him to Robert Piguet, who bought a few designs from him before commissioning a number of dresses. In 1938 Dior started working for Piguet as a designer. Piguet was known as "the prince of fashion" and ran one of the major fashion houses in Paris. The following year, war broke out and Dior had to report to the army in Mehun-sur-Yèvre, in the Cher region. He spent a year in the countryside, amidst local Berrichon farmers dressed in clogs. Nothing happened. It was "this strange war," during which he turned his attention to the cycle of the seasons and the growth patterns of plant life. The *débâcle* in 1940 allowed him to reach the South of France, where he joined his family in Callian. "Having discovered… that I too was a farmer, my sister and I decided to cultivate the small plot of land that surrounded the house." Every morning, Christian and Catherine picked flowers that they would sell at the market in Cannes, alongside peas and green beans. He was now responsible for his family, and they needed to survive.

When Piguet asked him to return to work, Dior hesitated, reluctant to see Paris under German occupation. By the time he made up his mind to go back, in 1941, the position had been filled. Piguet had hired someone else, but Lucien Lelong offered Dior a job, along with a certain Pierre Balmain, and the two learned the couturier trade. When Balmain left Lelong to open his own couture house, Dior began to think about doing the same.

One day, as he was out walking with his friend Pierre Colle, he stopped in front of 30 Avenue Montaigne, struck by the simplicity and beauty of this fine mansion. He joked that if he ever decided to set up on his own, it would be here, and nowhere else.

Christian Dior was superstitious. When he was fourteen years old, he attended a charity fair in Granville to benefit soldiers, where he met a clairvoyant: "You will find yourself penniless," she told him, "but women are good for you, and will bring you success. They will bring you great profit and you will travel widely." His superstition stayed with him through good times and bad. While hesitating about going to a meeting with Marcel Boussac, a textile magnate who needed a new director for his fashion house, Dior tripped on a small metal star. Taking it as a sign, he picked up the star, put it in his pocket, and set off for his appointment. Marcel Boussac was "curt and clear in style and speech, but had a truly kindly smile that softened his severity... Sitting across from this famous man, I suddenly understood my true plans... I quickly realized that we could get along very well."

With the eloquent bluntness of the genuinely shy, Christian Dior blurted to Boussac that he did not want to revive an existing company, he was looking to create his own in a location of his choice: "A fashion house where everything would be new, from the attitude and the staff to the furniture and the location... I was describing the fashion house of my dreams. It would be very small, very exclusive, with just a few ateliers, adopting the highest couture traditions for a select group of truly elegant women. My designs would look simple, but the couture would be highly elaborate." It was time for French couture to revert to the grand tradition of luxury. When Dior finally stopped talking, Boussac told him that this all seemed very well and good, but it was not the purpose of the meeting. Straight afterwards, however, Dior was told that Boussac found the project appealing.

Dior telephoned Boussac to apologize for his boldness and to say that he didn't really mean a word of what he had said; he also sent a telegram canceling their appointment. Was he afraid of the possibilities, or did he suddenly remember his promise to his mother, never to use the Dior name? "At that point, I went to see Madame D.... who had doggedly predicted that my sister would return from deportation. 'Accept it,' she said, 'accept it! You must create the House of Christian Dior!'" He called Boussac again to say he was ready to open his own couture house. Boussac agreed to all terms, and Dior moved into the building of his dreams at 30 Avenue Montaigne. The previous tenant, a milliner, had moved out just the day before: Dior saw this as another sign of his destiny.

The newborn House of Dior had a warm and welcoming atmosphere. All of Dior's friends were involved. A mood of confidence, excitement, good humor, and elation reigned. Christian Dior was never without his lucky star, his four-leaf clover, two hearts, a gold coin, and a piece of wood he touched constantly. His sister returned at the end of the war, just as the clairvoyant had repeatedly promised. If miracles were possible, so was magic. Dior would consult Madame D. for the rest of his life.

A New World

as he entered this brand-new world, Christian Dior remained true to what he loved. Flower arrangements recalled Granville, the walls and furniture echoed Passy and the eighteenth-century French style. The designs he sketched bore no resemblance to styles of the time, they evoked bygone days, the sweet days of his childhood, when elegance was paramount. His own past and culture formed a treasure trove of inspiration, sparked by images of a beautiful world, a contented, prosperous time when people went happily about their lives. He had been shocked by the harshness and darkness of war and dreamed of giving women back a lightheartedness they had all but forgotten. He wanted them to feel carefree, full of the joys of life he found so adorable and so essential. "We were coming out of a time of war, of uniforms and women soldiers... I designed flower-women with soft shoulders, ample necklines, tightly nipped waists, and wide, corolla-like skirts. But something so apparently delicate demanded rigorous construction. To meet my requirements for the precise cut and shape of the garment, I had to create an entirely new technique. I wanted my dresses to be 'constructed,' molded onto the contours of the female body, stylizing its curves. I emphasized the waistline and the breadth of the hips; I enhanced the bust. To give the clothing more volume, I lined all the fabrics with percale or taffeta, returning to a tradition that had long been overlooked." Dior also turned to sewing techniques of the past, and when need be, he and his team invented new ones. He wanted to offer women a heightened sense of femininity, happiness, and elegance. The extravagant quantities of fabric were a whiplash reaction to years of hardship and going without. In the words of the writer François Baudot, "Dior's New Look was the opposite of Chanel's look. It was the eternal comeback of the absolute woman—a queen, a star, or a pinup, celebrating the newfound abundance in a blaze of fireworks. The Liberation has no time for Coco's designs, fit for an 'underfed telegraph operator'."

Although he was deep in Proustian nostalgia, Dior's vision for women was decidedly oriented toward the future—a future he was creating for femininity itself. The Corolle line of his first collection was his way of re-creating a magnificent garden of dazzling flowers.

The very first Dior fashion show was held on February 12, 1947, in the salons of 30 Avenue Montaigne. Jean Cocteau, Dior's lifelong friend, was in attendance, as were Christian Bérard and Victor Grandpierre, who was the talented interior designer responsible for Dior's "Helleu" salons in white and pearl gray, and the Colifichets boutique, styled as an eighteenth-century fancy goods store; also present was Carmel Snow, the editor of *Harper's Bazaar*, who had been following Dior's progress for some time, having recognized him as the talent behind Lelong's most beautiful creations. Christian Dior revolutionized fashion with the Bar suit, which epitomized the entire line of this "New Look"—a name coined by Snow at the end of the show. The suit displayed the extent of Dior's masterful talent: A full, flouncing skirt paired with an architecturally structured jacket, which hugged the shoulders, cinched the waist, and padded the hips thanks to its basque pockets. The suit was molded and crafted to show off the female body. The tiny wasp waist was emblematic of the couturier's vision, eager for women to enjoy their figures again. Dior waited backstage: "Almost immediately, each model was applauded. I covered my ears, as the first bravos are always frightening. I didn't dare believe it, but a series of short reports suggested that my troops were winning… After the last dress was met with enthusiasm, Madame Marguerite, Madame Bricard, and I looked at each other, speechless. Raymonde came to get us, weeping with joy, and pushed us into the salon, where we were greeted with thunderous applause and bravos. Whatever joy may come my way in the future, nothing will ever surpass what I felt at that moment."

The New Look was a bombshell in the fashion world. Women ordered thirty dresses at a time. The House of Christian Dior became an instant legend; its success was such that between 1947 and 1954, the team grew from ninety people to nine hundred, and the number of ateliers rose from three to twenty-eight.

As a consolation for the recent hard times and to revive the splendor of the past, glamorous society balls were held. Christian Bérard hosted the Bal du Panache, Étienne de Beaumont held the Bal des Rois et Reines, and Charles de Beistegui chose the Palazzo Labia, in Venice, as the venue for his magnificent eighteenth-century-themed masked ball. Christian Dior played his part in all of them: "These festivities are actual works of art. They can be irritating by their very sumptuousness, but they are necessary, desirable, and important because they rekindle the taste and appreciation for authentic popular celebrations." Dior created legendary ball gowns for these events. The House of Dior benefited handsomely from what Dior called "the return to an ideal of civilized pleasure."

The Dior Vision

t o create and develop his couture house, Christian Dior drew on the legacy of European culture and refinement: Avenue Montaigne, the court of Versailles, grand Parisian parties, painters' palettes, the French art de vivre— all were natural sources of inspiration for him. He offered his clients so much more than wonderful clothes; he created the first global fashion house dedicated to refined luxury and the sophistication of Western civilization.

Following the phenomenal success of Dior's first collection, the world was his for the asking, and he wanted to be in charge of his expanding business. As of 1948, he established a couture atelier in New York. Americans were crazy for Dior, as was South America. The eyes of the world were riveted on Dior. Even the Communists sent a special delegation from the Moscow House of Designs to see his creations. For years Russian women wore clothes that were inspired by Dior patterns—though they didn't know it! Christian Dior was a savvy businessman and he established himself on every continent. He dressed the world's most beautiful women: The Duchess of Windsor, Princess Margaret, Marlene Dietrich, Jane Russell, Rita Hayworth, Marilyn Monroe, and Lauren Bacall were among his fervent admirers. Marlene Dietrich, who wore Dior both on-screen and off, for "the cut and the look," demanded that her entire wardrobe for Hitchcock's *Stage Fright* be designed by Dior. In March 1957, Dior received the ultimate consecration: He was the first couturier ever to be featured on the cover of *Time* magazine.

C elebrated around the world, Christian Dior was as respected by his coworkers as he was by his clients. He was passionate about the quality of his products and worked hand in hand with the most talented artisans of the time on all the house's creations, from the dresses to the embroideries, perfumes, and jewelry. He inspired the incomparable expertise of the dressmaking workshops, where he personally oversaw every detail.

In addition to being a man of extraordinary talent, who aspired to excellence in all aspects of his work, Christian Dior possessed great human qualities. He was attentive and generous to his staff, and in return they were very fond of their "boss." "He was a very elegant man. I never heard him raise his voice," said Pierre Cardin, head of the Dior tailoring atelier at the time. Dior cultivated friendships and remained close to the heart of his company; he had profound respect for all the seamstresses and assistants, whose work he appreciated like no other. He was especially devoted to the four women who worked with him and supported him from the start: Marguerite Carré, Suzanne Luling, Raymonde Zehnacker, and Mitzah Bricard, the "Joint Chiefs of Class," as he referred to them. Marguerite was his "second self" in matters of couture, for whom he invented the post of Technical Director. She was rigorous, understood everything, interpreted his designs to a tee, and served as the ideal intermediary between Monsieur Dior's "bureau of dreams" and the ateliers where they came to life. Suzanne, a childhood friend from Granville who was "full of life and enthusiasm," was practically a member of the family. She was in charge of public relations, receiving the Parisian elite in her apartment on the Quai Malaquais. Raymonde, his treasured right-hand woman, "took care of everything else." As for Mitzah, in Dior's own words she was "one of those rare people nowadays, who make elegance their sole raison d'être." Her "inimitable extremes" and flamboyant personality were a perfect balance to Dior's calm, typically Norman character. She was his "touch of folly," who cast a keen eye over the hats and accessories. While her somewhat pompous personality riled some, Dior was quick to stand up for her. He adored her; she was his muse.

To work on the looks and sketches for the following season, Dior liked to get away from Paris and head to one of his other homes: Le Moulin de Coudret mill house, in Milly-la-Forêt, near Fontainebleau, or the Château de la Colle Noire in Montauroux, in the Var region. There he would return to the pleasures of gardening, for flowers and nature had always been the great loves of his life.

Body and Line

most couturiers repeated their style from one season to the next, creating variations on the same theme. Christian Dior proposed an inimitable style, yet dreamed up a totally new silhouette for each collection and did not hesitate to reinvent his ideas every time. It was revolutionary. Dior's designs "set the style," and the fashion world would ferret for information about what would appear in the next new collection.

As a young man, Dior had not been mistaken about his vocation for architecture; he was indeed an architect, seeking harmony and coherence in the lines of his designs. He constructed dresses, molding them to the curves of a woman's body. He skimmed over the parts of the body he deemed less graceful—knees, shoulders, elbows—to create sheer beauty and an idealized shape. The new longer hemline "added mystery to the legs." The year after he presented his Corolle (Corolla) and En Huit (Figure 8) lines, he offered a new, flowing, sketchlike figure in the Zig-Zag line. The unevenly distributed fullness of the clothes in the Envol (Flight) line caused them to fly up then plunge down with each step the wearer took. In the 1948 Fall-Winter collection, he presented the Ailée (Winged) line, with a newly shaped sleeve that gave the impression of a wing and emphasized the bustline; it was a youthful and carefree style. In Spring-Summer 1949, he redesigned the female figure with trompe-l'œil features. Milieu de Siècle (Mid-Century), presented for the Fall-Winter collection of 1949, based the cut on the internal geometry of the fabric. Biased and straight lines intersected like scissors or radiated like windmills. Waists were cinched while the bust was boosted. The *coupe-vent* (windbreaker) collars made their first appearance: Raised in a triangular design, they framed the face. For Fall-Winter 1952, the Profilée (Profile) line was young and sharp, slimming and elongating the body. Tulipe (Tulip), the following year's line, recalled a flower in bloom. A new type of dart raised the bosom. The H-line, presented two years later, started the trend of a smaller bustline. Vertical armholes and a flatter chest created the illusion of a longer torso. Shirt-jackets went down to the hips. Dior introduced several day-to-night outfits. At the following Spring-Summer show, Dior introduced the A-line, a free and flared shape, based on the intersection of two diagonal lines, an angle that could be the subject of a thousand variations. Here the play on undefined waistlines was the essential feature, while sleeves were short or absent. In the Y-line, the waist was "more than tight," thereby "dramatically lengthening" both the skirt and the legs. Necklines were simple and often accompanied by a chemisette; sleeves were almost always long.

For Dior, a dress was "an ephemeral architecture designed to exalt the proportions of a woman's body." To achieve his incomparable silhouette, women returned to corsets and girdles. Some protested, but most had only one name running through their minds: Dior.

Pierre Cardin was twenty years old when he joined the House of Dior on its first day in business: December 16, 1946. Four years later, when Cardin expressed the desire to strike out on his own, Dior was supportive and introduced him to all the right people. "Everything I am, I owe to Christian Dior," he later said. Yves Saint Laurent also praised Dior: "Christian Dior was my master, the only one I acknowledge… His name will always be synonymous with French elegance." Dior chose Saint Laurent as his assistant in 1955. The young designer had been introduced to the couturier by Michel de Brunhoff, the editor of French *Vogue* and a long-term friend of Christian's, after seeing the sketches for which Saint Laurent had won first prize in the International Wool Secretariat contest. Many designers of extraordinary talent worked at Dior, including Frédéric Castet, a fur designer, who remained with the house until 1989, creating fantastic couture pieces that revolutionized the use of fur, and Roger Vivier, who reinvented the shoe for Dior.

Dior's sudden death in October 1957 caused great distress for all those who loved him and worked with him on a regular basis, as well as all his clients. The young Saint Laurent took over, creating an initial collection that kept close to the designs of the master. Named Trapèze (Trapeze), and inspired by the geometric lines that were so dear to Dior, the collection emphasized "equilibrium and construction." The new silhouette followed the lines of the trapezoid and owed its elegance to the simplicity and purity of the design. The Trapèze line became a fashion milestone by creating a totally new shape and dramatically shortening the hemline. When Saint Laurent was drafted into military service in Algeria, he was replaced by Marc Bohan, who had been creative director of Dior London. His very first collection was a success, with Elizabeth Taylor ordering a full twelve dresses. Princess Grace of Monaco swore by Dior; her daughter Caroline would become an equally ardent fan. Empress Farah Diba had a Dior coat made for her coronation. Marc Bohan remained creative director of the House of Dior for the next twenty-nine years. After Bohan came Gianfranco Ferré. His style favored large collars and voluminous shapes, contrasting elements and highly structured silhouettes, reviving much of the Dior spirit.

By the mid-nineties, the fashion scene in England was buzzing, and John Galliano was one of its most celebrated names. The man who was as much a Spaniard from London as an Englishman from Gibraltar succeeded Ferré as creative director of the House of Dior in 1996. The first dress he designed was worn by Diana, Princess of Wales, for the opening of the Dior retrospective at the Metropolitan Museum of Art in New York. Princess Di proved to be the most prestigious fan of the Lady Dior handbag; she owned several, in different colors and sizes, and took them wherever she went. The handbag instantly became iconic.

John Galliano followed the Dior tradition. The master's spirit meshed well with the British designer's exotic creativity, magnifying and enhancing a mutual inspiration. The two designers shared many interests, notably the love of art, historical figures, and travel. Galliano would often choose one of Dior's lines or his favorite people and places to fire his own imagination. Dior admired Léon Bakst, the set and costume designer for the famous Ballets Russes; Galliano was obsessed with Bakst's close friend, the fabled Marchesa Casati, a supremely elegant lady of society, adding his own touches of fantasy to her extravagant style.

For his Fall-Winter collection of 2005, Galliano delved into the history of the company and its ateliers. His designs bore the names of Christian Dior's most famous models: Victoire, France, and Lucky. He also drew inspiration from the photographs of Irving Penn, Richard Avedon, Willy Maywald, and Henri Cartier-Bresson, all photographers who captured the essence of Dior fashion.

Artists were also a vivid source of inspiration for Galliano, as seen in his 2007 Fall-Winter collection, Le Bal des Artistes. Dior had named some of his designs Dalí, Cocteau, Boldini, or Bakst; Galliano continued the tradition by revisiting Boldini, so dear to Dior, and paying tribute to Malevich, Cocteau, Picasso, and the very talented Bérard, Dior's close friend.

The Fall-Winter collection of 2009 recalled the photographs Cartier-Bresson took in the 1950s of models backstage in the *cabine*, or fitting room. Dior and Galliano shared an interest in travel, and several exotic Haute Couture collections were inspired by study trips Galliano and his team took to Russia (Spring-Summer 2002), Egypt (Spring-Summer 2004), South America (Fall-Winter 2005), and Japan (Spring-Summer 2007).

John Galliano brought just the right amount of bold fantasy to enter the new millennium. His flamboyant, dreamlike world harked back to the grand society balls that Dior so enjoyed. He drew avidly from this extraordinary heritage to produce a highly modern and creative interpretation. Galliano dared. He combined Dior's cherished *S* silhouette of the Belle Époque with the ornaments worn by the Masai tribe women. His version of the well-known necklace was the inspiration for the J'adore perfume bottle.

The Dior Codes

t he House of Dior's fashion codes are directly tied to its creator, his culture, taste, and vision. Dior gray was the color of his childhood apartment in Passy; pink was the color of his house in Granville; leopard print was the trademark of Mitzah Bricard. Other emblems of the brand include traditionally masculine fabrics used in women's clothing, such as houndstooth, Prince of Wales check, tweed, and polka dots, as well as the eighteenth-century armchair, Dior's lucky number 8, and the Médaillon chair designed by Riesener, who was Marie-Antoinette's cabinet-maker. Lily of the valley and roses, Monsieur Dior's favorite flowers, the *cannage* (cane-work) pattern used in Napoleon III chairs, the Fontange bow, and the CD monogram are just some of the couturier's distinctive symbols.

Today, the House of Dior's identity revolves around the same values of femininity, savoir faire, and respect for tradition, while looking resolutely toward the future. The Dior universe is a world unto itself, a world of endless possibilities filled with its own landmarks, references, and paths to new adventures and emotions: From the cannage motif to the good-luck charms that dangle from the iconic Lady Dior handbag, roses to lilies of the valley, the Belle Époque of Madeleine Dior to the Russian avant-garde, the Fontange bow to the flamboyant color red, and the extraordinary postwar society balls to the couturier's love of art, the world of Christian Dior is constantly evolving yet rooted in a rich and unique history that has made the Dior name mythical all across the world.

The House of Dior was built on its founder's astounding ability to embody elegance through his bold creations. His inventive essence is today upheld by the designers who succeed him. Their unparalleled originality and surprising audacity follow in Christian Dior's own footsteps, and it is thanks to their talents that the House of Dior continues to inspire international couture and launch iconic styles. In the twenty-first century, Dior must define modern elegance with the same bold spirit that animated the master when he launched his couture house.

Conclusion

his mother wanted him to be a diplomat, but Christian Dior became so much more. An ambassador indeed for the utmost in French refinement and sophistication, a legacy maintained by the couture house he created. Christian Dior was elegance incarnate. From his very first collection in 1947, he breathed new creativity into French luxury. He imposed his style around the world, became the couturier of princesses, and used his innate talent and style to build a refined, elite world of luxury that fires and inspires dreams. Dior not only makes women more beautiful, he makes them happier, and his became the most famous French name in the world. His friend Jean Cocteau described him as "this agile genius of our times, whose magical name contains Dieu [God] and Or [gold]." The House of Dior today continues its founder's tradition of innovation and artistry. In the twenty-first century, as in 1947, Dior style inspires the dreams and desires of women throughout the world.

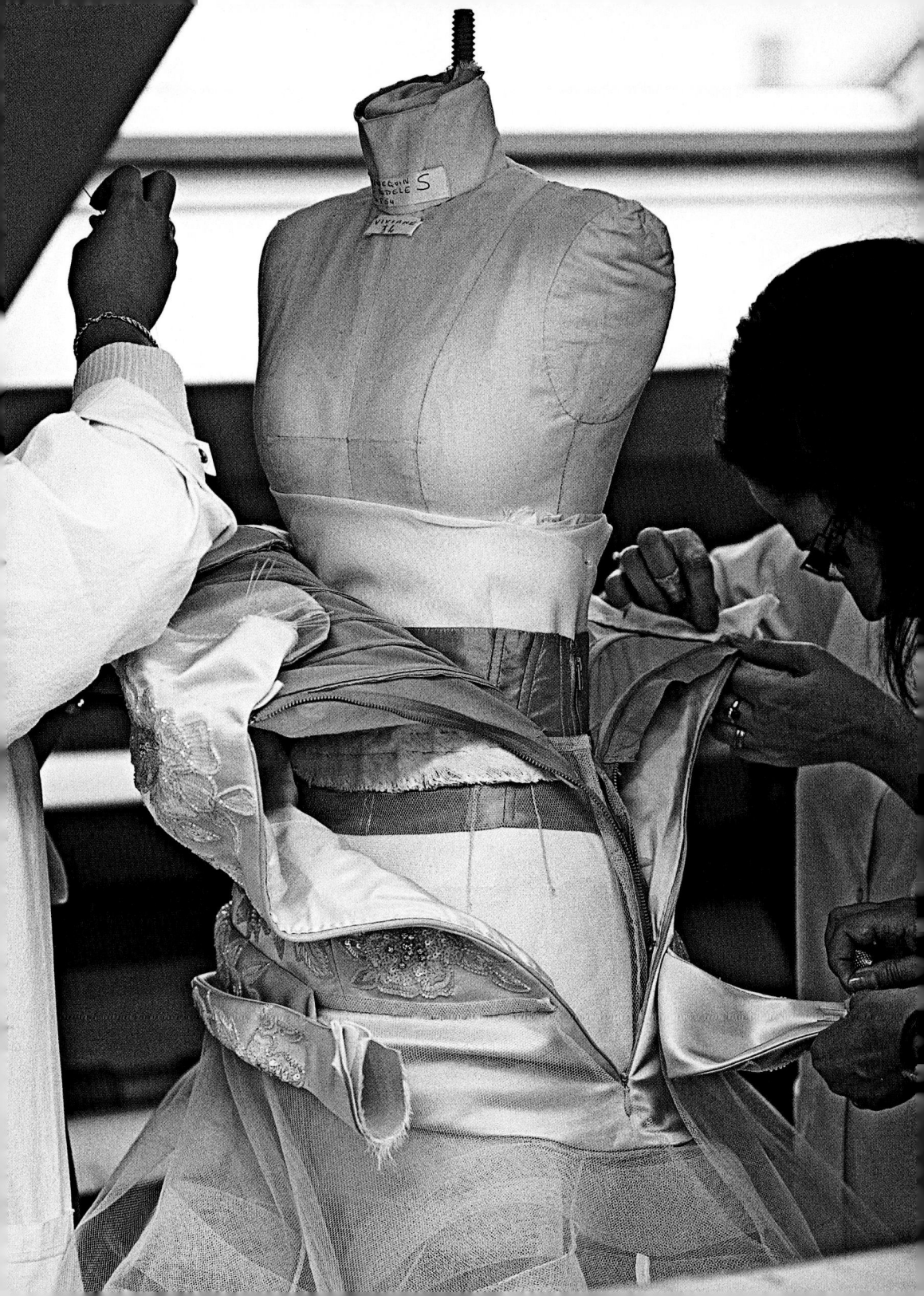

66 Great parties are a necessity because they bring joy. 99

Theo Graham, dress by Dior, Pré Catelan, Paris, August 1949.
Photograph by Richard Avedon.

1. The Begum Aga Khan and Rita Hayworth at Dior, circa 1949.
2. Christian Dior and Jane Russell, 1954.
3. Pablo Picasso in the sculpture room, 1966. Photo: Roberto Otero.
4. Carmel Snow and Louise Dahl-Wolfe at Dior.
5. Ava Gardner and Christian Dior at the fitting for *The Little Hut*, 1957.
6. The Duchess of Windsor at Dior.
7. Ingrid Bergman in *Indiscreet*, 1958.
8. The Saphir dress, from the Fall-Winter 1949 Haute Couture collection.
9. Marlene Dietrich at Dior, circa 1950.
10. Salvador Dalí with Amanda Lear.
11. The collective exhibition *Surrealism: Sculptures, Objects, Paintings, and Drawings* at Galerie Pierre Colle, June 1933. Photo: Man Ray.
12. Christian Dior and Olivia de Havilland, for the film *The Ambassador's Daughter*, in 1955.
13. Princess Margaret visiting the House of Dior, 1951.
14. Portrait of Alberto Giacometti surrounded by his sculptures, 1951. Photo: Gordon Parks.

66 The Duchess of Windsor
adores Paris, because Paris
is not far from Dior. 99

The Duke of Windsor

The Duchess of Windsor wearing Dior. Illustration by Kenneth Paul Block, 1962.

TWENTY CENTS

MARCH 4, 1957

TIME

THE WEEKLY NEWSMAGAZINE

HIGH FASHION
The Paris Designers

CHRISTIAN
DIOR

Robert Vickrey

$6.00 A YEAR

VOL LXIX NO. 9

Chronology

1905: On January 21, Christian Dior is born in Granville; the family moves into the villa Les Rhumbs.

1946: December 16, the couture house is inaugurated at 30 Avenue Montaigne. The House of Christian Dior employs 90 people in its three ateliers, including Pierre Cardin.

1947: Presentation of the first Christian Dior collection, for Spring-Summer 1947, in the salons at 30 Avenue Montaigne. The Bar suit becomes the emblem of the New Look.

1950: Christian Dior is made a Chevalier de la Légion d'Honneur.

1951: Christian Dior writes his first book, *Je suis couturier*. The House of Christian Dior employs 900 people.

1953: Christian Dior launches a made-to-measure footwear line in collaboration with Roger Vivier.

1954: Christian Dior organizes a show at Blenheim Palace in England in honor of Princess Margaret. In Paris, the House of Christian Dior occupies five buildings—including 25 ateliers—and accounts for over half of French haute couture exports.

1955: Opening of the boutique at the corner of Avenue Montaigne and Rue François I. Christian Dior gives a lecture on the aesthetics of fashion to 4,000 students at the Sorbonne. Yves Saint Laurent is hired as Christian Dior's first assistant.

1956: Christian Dior publishes *Dior by Dior*.

1957: On March 4, *Time* magazine dedicates its cover to Christian Dior. Christian Dior hires Marc Bohan as creative director of Dior London. October 24, Christian Dior dies. Yves Saint Laurent is named creative director.

1958: Yves Saint Laurent's first collection for Christian Dior Haute Couture, Spring-Summer 1958.

1959: The Christian Dior Haute Couture collection is presented in Moscow for the first time, in front of an audience of 11,000.

1960: Marc Bohan becomes creative director of the house of Dior.

1967: Creation of the first Dior ready-to-wear collection, christened Miss Dior. Launch of the Baby Dior line and opening of the first Baby Dior boutique, inaugurated by HSH Princess Grace of Monaco.

1968: Frédéric Castet takes the helm of the fashion fur department.

1970: Marc Bohan creates the first Christian Dior Monsieur line.

Christian Dior graced the cover of *Time* magazine on March 4, 1957. The article inside called him fashion's "Dictator by Demand." © 2011 Time Inc., used under license.

1987: The 40th anniversary of the house of Christian Dior. A major retrospective, *Homage to Christian Dior 1947–1957*, is organized at the UCAD in Paris.

1989: Gianfranco Ferré succeeds Marc Bohan.

1992: Patrick Lavoix is appointed creative director of Christian Dior Monsieur.

1995: Diana Princess of Wales opens the Cézanne exhibition sponsored by LVMH and Christian Dior at the Grand Palais, and is presented with the first Lady Dior bag by Mme Jacques Chirac.

1996: John Galliano succeeds Gianfranco Ferré as creative director.
For the 50th anniversary of the House, an exhibition, *Christian Dior*, is organized at the Metropolitan Museum of Art in New York City. At the opening, Diana Princess of Wales wears the first dress created by John Galliano for Dior.

1997: First Haute Couture collection created by John Galliano, for Spring-Summer 1997. Christian Dior Museum is inaugurated in Granville on June 10.

1998: Victoire de Castellane becomes creator of the Christian Dior Fine Jewellery line.

1999: A new Dior boutique opens on 57th Street in New York City.

2000: Hedi Slimane is named creative director of Dior Homme.

2004: Charlize Theron wins the Golden Globe for Best Actress for her film *Monster*. She wears a dress created specially by John Galliano for Dior.

2007: The Haute Couture Fall-Winter 2007 collection is presented at the Orangerie at Versailles, celebrating the 60th anniversary of the house of Dior and 10 years of creation by John Galliano for Christian Dior.
Kris Van Assche is named creative director of Dior Homme.

2008: Marion Cotillard, winner of an Academy Award for her interpretation of Edith Piaf in the film *La Vie en Rose*, directed by Olivier Dahan, becomes a new Dior muse.
Opening of the exhibition *Christian Dior and Chinese Artists* in Beijing.

2009–2010: Marion Cotillard stars in promotional videos for the Lady Dior handbag: "The Lady Noire Affair," directed by Olivier Dahan; "Lady Rouge," directed by Jonas Åkerlund, featuring Marion Cotillard performing the song "Eyes of Mars," by Franz Ferdinand; "Lady Blue Shanghai," directed by David Lynch; and "Lady Grey London," directed by John Cameron Mitchell.

2010: First Dior fashion show presented in China, in Shanghai.

2011: On April 26, inauguration of the exhibition *Inspiration Dior* at the Pushkin State Museum of Fine Art in Moscow.
Launch of the Dior VIII watch.

A shoe design from the Winter 2010 collection. Photo © Philippe Lacombe.

Dior

The Haute Couture ateliers. These legendary workshops are the heart and soul of the House of Dior. Faithful to Christian Dior's vision, *premières* and *petites mains* display a unique savoir faire, continually pushing the boundaries of craftsmanship to produce marvelous creations. The famed photographer Patrick Demarchelier brought some of these artisans together in front of 30 Avenue Montaigne for a spread in American *Vogue*, October 2008. Photo © Patrick Demarchelier/*Vogue*/Condé Nast Publications.

Artists and Christian Dior. A gallerist at just 22, Dior exhibited Giacometti, Dalí, Calder, and many others. He had a special friendship with Christian Bérard, and this drawing shows the artist's affection for his friend the great couturier. Left: Bérard's "Hommage à Christian Dior," 1947, © 2011 Artists Rights Society (ARS), New York/ADAGP, Paris. Right: Dior and Bérard at Milly-la-Forêt, 1946. Photo: Louise Dahl-Wolfe/Collection Center for Creative Photography, University of Arizona © 1989 Arizona Board of Regents.

30 Avenue Montaigne. The couturier chose this address in 1946 as his headquarters, for its simple proportions and quiet, refined elegance. Left: Christian Dior surrounded by hats, gloves, muffs, lingerie, hosiery, evening bags, and jewelry, circa 1955. Photo © Hulton Archive/Getty Images. Right: A portrait of Christian Dior by Bernard Buffet hanging in the boutique at 30 Avenue Montaigne. Photo © Jimmy Cohrssen.

Christian Dior and the 18th century. Christian Dior had a particular affinity for the 18th-century French court style of Louis XVI and Marie-Antoinette. He loved to decorate with a mixture of styles and eras, calling it true modernity. He dubbed this style "Louis XVI–1910," and his friend Victor Grandpierre humorously referred to it as "Louis Dior." Left: Watercolor of Dior's salon at Avenue Montaigne by Garance Wilkens. Right: Christian Dior at home. Photo © Cecil Beaton/Camera Press.

Illustrator and designer. Christian Dior's drawings were his entrée into the world of fashion, and drawing for magazines and designing for couturiers Robert Piguet and Lucien Lelong prepared him to launch his own eponymous house. Left: Christian Dior sketching designs at his worktable. Photo © Émile Savitry/Gamma Rapho. Right: Watercolor by Garance Wilkens of the Dior house models in the couture salon.

Technical excellence. The House of Dior combines a heritage of traditional techniques with modern technology, a marriage of artistry and craftsmanship that pushes the limits of fantasy in the service of unfailing excellence. One dress can entail up to a thousand hours of work. Left: Model Stella Tennant in *Vogue Italia*, March 2010, wearing the France dress from the Fall-Winter 2005 Haute Couture collection by John Galliano. Photo © Tim Walker/Art + Commerce. Right: Spring-Summer 2010 Haute Couture collection. Photo © Sophie Carre.

The Lady Dior bag in red crocodile. Photo © Laziz Hamani.

Exaggerated femininity . The Corolle and En Huit lines of Christian Dior's first collection—the New Look—revolutionized fashion after the end of World War II, transforming the female silhouette by changing its proportions and cinching the waistline. Left: A look from Dior's debut Spring-Summer 1947 collection, from British *Vogue*, 1947. Photo © Clifford Coffin/trunkarchive.com. Right: Marion Cotillard wearing a dress from the Spring-Summer 2010 prêt-à-porter collection by John Galliano. Photo © Craig McDean/Art + Commerce.

Mitzah, the muse. Mitzah Bricard, Christian Dior's closest friend and adviser, brought her stylish touch to the house's hats and accessories. She was most fond of leopard print and the color lilac, which she wore almost every day. Dior said she was "one of those rare people nowadays for whom elegance is their sole raison d'être." She was his muse, and he adored her. Left: Mitzah Bricard by Cecil Beaton, courtesy of the Cecil Beaton Studio Archive at Sotheby's. Right: Fall-Winter 2009 Haute Couture collection. Photo © Sophie Carre.

Society balls. After the war, many extravagant costume balls were thrown—such as the Bal des Rois et Reines hosted by Count Étienne de Beaumont, which Dior attended dressed as a lion—bringing back the pageantry of former times. Christian Dior loved taking part in them, deeming them true works of art, and the dresses he created for them were legendary. The House of Dior profited from what the couturier called "a return of peoples' spirits to an ideal of civilized happiness." Photo © Keystone France/Gamma Keystone via Getty Images.

Versailles and aristocracy. The grandeur of Versailles during the reign of Marie-Antoinette was a source of infinite inspiration for Christian Dior. The world of the noble court of the 18th century profoundly influenced the couturier's style and his approach to luxury. Left: The France dress, photographed at Versailles, 1951. Photo © Association Willy Maywald/Artists Rights Society (ARS), New York/ADAGP, Paris. Right: Lauren Bush wearing the Mitzah gown from the Fall-Winter 2005 Haute Couture collection by John Galliano at the Hôtel de Crillon in Paris for the Bal des Débutantes, December 2000. Photo © Chomel/Sipa.

Flower gardens. "The garden that nurtured my childhood" is how Dior described the gardens of the villa where he grew up in Granville. When he became a couturier he dreamed of "flower women," and more than 50 of his creations were named for flowers. This theme inspired John Galliano's Florale line for Fall-Winter 2010, in homage to the Tulipe line from Spring-Summer 1953, and was presented at the Musée Rodin gardens. Left: © Mats Gustafson/Art + Commerce. Right: © Sophie Carre.

The New Look. In 1947 Christian Dior revolutionized fashion with the Bar suit, which summed up the New Look. Composed of a wide twirling skirt and a structured jacket with fitted shoulders and tightly cinched waist, molded to accentuate the female form, the Bar suit is the most modern of classics, constantly reinterpreted in new ways, such as this fringed jacket (left) designed by John Galliano in 1997. Left: © Laziz Hamani. Right: © Karl Lagerfeld.

Menswear fabrics. From the very beginning of his couture house, Christian Dior adopted traditional menswear fabrics to give a unique cachet and impart a sophisticated elegance to his fashions for women. Houndstooth, Prince of Wales plaid, tennis stripes, and tweed became part of the vocabulary of womenswear and have been signatures of the House of Dior, inspiring the master's successors, including Marc Bohan, as seen in these designs from 1964. Photo © Frank Horvat/Condé Nast Archives/Corbis.

The Lady Dior handbag. The Lady Dior bag was born in 1995, presented by French first lady Bernadette Chirac to Princess Diana, who never went anywhere without it. A marvel of savoir faire, the now legendary Lady Dior bag is both mythical and modern, inspiring the biggest names in contemporary art. Here, interpretations from the exhibition *Lady Dior As Seen By*, in Shanghai in 2011. Left: Lady Dior As Seen By Ben Hassett. Right: Lady Dior As Seen By Olympia Scarry.

Dior

PERFUME

To my mother, who only ever wore Miss Dior.

Slipcase front: Detail of an advertisement for Miss Dior perfume, illustrated
by René Gruau. Photo © SARL René Gruau/www.renegruau.com.
Slipcase back: *Dovima with elephants, evening dress by Dior, Cirque
d'Hiver, Paris, August 1955*. Photo © The Richard Avedon Foundation.
Following pages: The first Christian Dior amphora
perfume bottle, 1947. Photo © Laziz Hamani.
© 2012 Assouline Publishing
601 West 26th Street, 18th floor
New York, NY 10001, USA
Tel.: 212-989-6810   Fax: 212-647-0005
www.assouline.com
Color separation by Luc Alexis Chasleries.
Text translated from the French by Gail de Courcy-Ireland.
Captions written by Vincent Leret.
Printed in China.
ISBN: 9781614280286

Jérôme Hanover

Dior

PERFUME

ASSOULINE

> **❝ All of Dior's perfumes uphold their initial legacy: to be very couture, very Dior. ❞**

a thick white mantle cloaks the setting; Avenue Montaigne seems to want to match the sable coats of the elegant ladies hurrying down it. Paris is covered in snow. Just one week ago, temperatures dropped to 7° Fahrenheit. At number 30, the atmosphere is heady with excitement: In a matter of days, Christian Dior will present his first haute couture show, and his team is busy making sure it will be as perfect as Monsieur wants it. "Will he make his mark?" is the question no doubt running through everybody's minds, from the seamstress stitching earnestly away, to the couturier, stressed by the stakes at play. We now know that February 12, 1947, would go down in history, but at the time uncertainty reigned. Christian Dior had a new vision of women: not simply of the female figure, but of a woman's presence overall. Haute couture would dress her, while perfume would accompany her, lingering in her wake. Sometimes it would even precede her: In his new store, where the final adjustments were being made for the upcoming opening, a full liter of perfume would be sprayed every week—the very fragrance that would cast its spell over Dior's salons during the couture event of the year, which posterity has recorded as the New Look. Perfume would complement Dior's vision of style, it would be its prolongation in scent—more still, its match. Christian Dior took such care and time over this fragrance, no one could underrate its significance in relation to fashion. The two would progress side by side, in mutual enrichment and inspiration. In the pearl-gray salons on the third floor, Christian Dior's mind was racing. With the last fittings came the final tweaks to the dresses. Small questions could not turn into big issues, yet still there was no name for this perfume, a floral green chypre. Within a few dozen hours, this new fragrance would be to perfumery what the first Dior couture show became to fashion, but the reason it was still being referred to by its code name was not for discretion's sake. A thousand words jostled in Christian Dior's head, already adding to the overexertion that would strike him down ten years later. Which to choose? Mitzah Bricard was pacing up and down. She was his muse, his advisor, his paragon of elegance, the caryatid he could count on for support. Catching Christian's eye in the mirror above the grand marble chimneypiece, she paused to check her profile, queenly as Nefertiti. She was wearing her ubiquitous leopard-print scarf, knotted around her wrist like a *tabaquero* singing *Carmen,* a touch of brazen irony in contrast with her elegant natural allure, as if to snub the diamonds and pearls nestled beneath her blouse. The door opened a crack, quiet and discreet, typical of Catherine Dior, as she slipped in to see her brother on some long-forgotten pretext. Christian snapped out of his musing and smiled; all stress seemed to subside. He was her "Tian" and she his darling "chérie." Mademoiselle Dior. Twelve years his junior. Mitzah Bricard, whose mother was English, rose from her Médaillon chair: "Ah, here's Miss Dior!" she exclaimed. Miss Dior? Miss Dior! All was ready: The show could go on. "Outfit number one…"

❝ Christian Dior's legacy to the house he founded is a creative universe, a vision of perfumery intimately linked to his fashion. ❞

Miss Dior is a perfume manifesto, but not simply because it was the House of Dior's first fragrance. It clearly states the couturier's intention to turn perfumery into a fashion accessory, an indispensable item of luxury. Since its creation, over seventy other fragrances or variations have been born.

From eaux de toilette to absolutes, colognes to extracts, all of Dior's perfumes uphold their initial legacy: to be very couture, very Dior.

"Perfume is the indispensable complement to the personality of women, the finishing touch on a dress."[1] In Christian Dior's wildest dreams, he would have been able to create a fragrance for each of the looks in his couture show. This couldn't happen, of course, for fashion and perfumery play on very different time scales.[2] Yet the ultimate fantasy has been transposed within the House of Dior through a very clear bond between the two departments. Yards of exceptional materials for one, a rigorous selection of the most precious ingredients for the other.[3] In the postwar years when going without—be it clothes or perfumes—was still an everyday reality for French ladies, Christian Dior reinvented luxury and dreams. This new statement required a new language. His perfume was like his vision of fashion: iconoclastic, imposing accords and constructions that often flouted the prevailing perfumery canons. Yet just as his New Look broke with the fashion of the day to draw inspiration from the dresses of the Belle Époque, his fragrances traveled back in time to fully translate the influence of perfume history into a modern olfactory language. So it was for Diorissimo. When it arrived on the pearl-gray shelves of Dior boutiques in 1956, this perfume composed by Edmond Roudnitska both inspired and enthralled. Youngsters loved the fragrance: It was like nothing they had ever known. "I worked with fresh, light notes, clear and flowing, purely olfactory, and avoiding any heavy, gustative effects," explained the perfume's creator. "I monitored each link between the different accords to bring out a kind of olfactory melody and ensure an overall unity to the perfume's form."[4] Diorissimo goes straight to the heart; it is a clean, absolute floral. "It opens with fresh green notes of soil and crumpled leaves that hook you in. A clear, clean *sillage* takes over. The theme is an armful of lily of the valley. It intoxicates, plays on jasmine, orange blossom, rose, and lilac, becoming heady and more intense, heavier and more sensual, deeper and more animal. There is a form of olfactory expression, signature, and style that shines forth beyond the theme. The components are mastered and contain a perfect sequence, a deep olfactory knowledge of a sprig of lily of the valley, picked at dawn and inhaled until the evening."[5] As a perfume narrative that spins the story of a day in the flower's life, Diorissimo instantly put all the heavy, grandiloquent constructions of its peers out of fashion: It is a romantic fragrance with a tight, coherent vocabulary, a perfume that could have been made in the nineteenth century. At the time, the absence of gustative notes (vanilla, sweet, or fruity) stood out against most contemporary creations because its pedigree traveled even further back in time, to the days before synthetic molecules.[6] "I decided to break with most of the products that had been overused," concluded Edmond Roudnitska about Diorissimo.[7] Didn't Christian Dior have the very same thing in mind when revolutionizing and redefining the female figure in each of his couture shows?

From then on, the visual identity had to be the same for both worlds. While this approach can today seem self-evident in a fragrance market heavily influenced by fashion labels, which see perfumes as an extension of their textile proposal, back in the postwar years, when the first Dior perfumes were born, it was far from obvious. Christian Dior was not the first couturier to feel he was a perfumer: Nina Ricci, Pierre Balmain, Cristobal Balenciaga, Gabrielle Chanel, and others had created perfumes, and Elsa Schiaparelli even chose names for each of her fragrances that started with her own initial (Shocking, Snuff, Souci, Salut…) and stamped her signature pink throughout. But for most of the above, the only thing that was couture about a perfume was its luxuriousness and its name. Christian Dior thought otherwise. Although his fragrances were an olfactory translation of his fashion world, for most women this correlation was rather esoteric. To know it, you had to see it. Posed majestically on pleated gray silk, the womanly curves of the original Miss Dior bottle, designed by Fernand Guéry-Colas in 1947, seem to highlight a hipline magnified by the basque of a Bar suit. In 1950, a new design asserted the influence from fashion even more distinctly: The geometrically structured, square-shaped bottle was inspired by the Vertical line.[8] Its frosted glass reproduces the houndstooth motif favored by Christian Dior, an originally masculine check to which he brought feminine grace and sensuality. A pretty couture bow adorns the bottle neck: All the House of Dior codes are there, as though the perfume itself is dressed in Dior. Taking the analogy of perfumes as dresses further, Christian Dior blended them into the world of couture by having their bottles echo the atmosphere and details in the salons at 30 Avenue Montaigne, like a string of mini-boutiques. The dominant Trianon gray and white, the medallion inspired by the backs of the neo–Louis XVI chairs… The black and white packaging of Eau Fraîche may seem a far cry from the *cannage*, or cane-work, on the concert-hall chairs in Dior Haute Couture shows, yet it adopts the rattan furniture motif of which the couturier was so fond. The exact Napoleon III weave motif has been honored on the different Escales bottles since 2008.[9] And when the people at Dior imagined a new version of Miss Dior Chérie in 2011, they made the couture identity clearly apparent, all the way down to the stylized embroidery on the perfume's posters and packaging.

> A pretty couture bow adorns the bottle neck: All the House of Dior codes are there, as though the perfume itself is dressed in Dior.

"Naturally, the dress can correspond to the name it bears... but these christenings have not always been purposefully thought out," Christian Dior explained. "The dresses start out with a number; we don't name them until they start to come to life, in order to differentiate them the further they are in the making."[10] Indeed, the name the couturier gave should not be interpreted as a literal description. More than one dress or outfit has been named Rosée, meaning "dew" in

French, which seems to evoke the fresh morning dewdrops in a garden—yet they have all been evening wear. We could argue that the lady may have danced the night away in her organdy dress stitched with *broderie anglaise*, only returning home at dawn, or that Christian Dior was perhaps playing on the irony in this paradox.[11] We could even imagine the drops of dew that appear on plants and flowers in the first flush of day, as though having drunk their scent all night long: Is this not the perfect metaphor for perfume? But fun as it may be to hypothesize on the interpretation of this or that name the couturier father gave his fashion offspring, it is the recurring vocabulary from the Dior lexicon, collection after collection, which tells us most about Christian Dior's intentions. In the decade from 1947 to 1957, over three hundred couture outfits bore a name linked to perfumery, with flowers uppermost among them—the flowers that compose the house fragrances. The gardenia and patchouli found in Miss Dior are also a day suit and an afternoon dress respectively.[12] The mandarin in Eau Fraîche gave its name, Mandarine, to a chiffon outfit and a black woolen coat.[13] The lily of the valley in Diorissimo, Muguet, has been a lingerie gown, a fur *paletot*, two evening gowns, and a short-skirted outfit.[14] There have been Acacia, Marguerite, Pétunia, Réséda, Myosotis, Lys, Iris, Coquelicot, Dahlia, Hortensia, Lupin, Œillet, Colza, Bouton d'or, Angélique, Scabieuse,[15] and an endless array of roses: Roseraie, Rosée, Rose de France, Damascus Rose, Christmas Rose, April or Brabant Rose, Tea Rose, Black Rose or Red Rose, Rose Pompon, Nuit Rose, Fête des Roses, Soirée Rose, Palais Rose, La Vie en Rose, and even Fontenay-aux-Roses—a southern suburb of Paris! Virtually every scented flower that exists seems to have lent its name to at least one Dior dress. In the elite haute couture that all women dream of but only few can wear, city flowers mix with country blooms: Sported prettily in a buttonhole, found in the wild during a stroll, planted in endless lush flowerbeds, simple or sophisticated; every flower is beautiful, Christian Dior seems to say, every flower smells lovely. To echo the names of these outfits that recall perfumery's soliflores—fragrances created around a single flower—he created his own bouquets and evocative compositions: his very own accords. Hence Jardin Japonais, or Japanese garden, which makes it so easy to imagine the scent of blossoming cherry trees, orchids, and lotus flowers behind this afternoon dress and coat.[16] And can't you just sense the winding ivy and fresh hollyhock in this wool suit and organza blouse named Charmille, the French for "arbor"?[17] In Herbier, a beige crepe dress with matching wool suit, whose name evokes the herbariums of old, can't you snatch the scent of crisp dried flowers pressed against yellowing paper? Not to mention the Jardin de Curé, literally "priest's garden" in French, which has been at once a black alpaca coat, an evening gown, and a dinner dress?[18] Does it not echo the famous Jardin de Mon Curé, created by Jacques Guerlain in 1895, and its accords of lemon, jasmine, and ylang-ylang? Dior even adorned his dresses with the names of his own perfumes, and vice versa: Miss Dior became a cocktail dress in black faille and an evening gown embroidered with a thousand flowers, while Diorama was a black wool dress trimmed with skunk before becoming Edmond Roudnitska's first perfume for Dior.[19] The name is sported by two other dresses too: one a surat cotton dinner dress and the other featuring a black horsehair trim against a pink background.[20] The connections have persisted well beyond the couturier's death: Jules, the name of a suit in 1956, became a masculine fragrance twenty-four years later. And Chérie, which was both a suit and a dress during Christian Dior's lifetime, became the new version of Miss Dior in 2005.[21]

Christian Dior loved playing with words, starting with his own name. Soft, rounded, sensual, and glamorous, it trips off the tongue, lingers on the diphthong, then melts into the final syllable. Dior is such a euphonic name, and Christian gave his surname to all his perfumes, as though claiming their paternity. First Miss Dior, in 1947, in reference to his sister Catherine, as we have seen. Then Diorama in 1949, which now seems so closely linked to the perfume we forget that the word was first imagined by Louis Daguerre in 1822 as the name for one of his inventions, the ancestor of film, whose special way of lighting translucent panels gave the illusion of motion to the scenes portrayed, and which comes from the Greek *dia*, meaning through, and *orama*, meaning sight. It is a couture perfume for the silver screen. In 1956, Diorissimo echoed the musical annotations pianissimo (very soft) or fortissimo (very loud). In Italian, the *–issimo* suffix is the superlative, so Diorissimo should be seen as pure Dior: Dior to the power of Dior! In fact, this was probably Christian Dior's most personal perfume, featuring lily of the valley, his favorite flower, which he made sure was sewn into the lining of his dresses to bring him luck in his couture shows. His involvement even stretched to designing the spectacular bottle and its stopper, which blooms like a great bouquet of gilded flowers. Yet this perfume was also his last. By 1963, both Christian Dior and Serge Heftler-Louiche, his childhood friend and cofounder of Parfums Christian Dior, had passed away, but the spirit lived on. A new fragrance was created by Paul Vacher, the nose behind Miss Dior, still playing on the master's name once more: Diorling rings like darling. Then came Diorella, as fresh and spicy as a young woman sparkling in couture; Dior-Dior, a double-barreled Dior; and Dioressence, the utmost essence of Dior, consummate femininity. In J'adore too, no doubt, there is still a play on the name, in *adioration* of the master.

eau Sauvage was the first masculine fragrance created by Dior. The first actually made for men, many of whom—including Christian Dior himself—had already adopted Eau Fraîche, a simple, natural cologne created by Edmond Roudnitska for Dior in 1955, whose advertising and packaging played on an ambiguity between his and hers and seemed to address both. Ladies saw it as a light and sporty summer fragrance, gentlemen as a subtle, invigorating *jus* that had shed the scent of lavender, at last! Eau Fraîche had become a unisex fragrance, no doubt the first to exist on such a scale, but it had been imagined as a women's eau de toilette: a light, citrus chypre that fit the tastes of American ladies in the 1950s. When Edmond Roudnitska created Eau Sauvage thirteen tears later, he wanted to take the perfumery theory he had elaborated in creating Diorissimo—clean rigor and more olfactory notes than gustative—and apply it to men. "The characteristic of Eau Sauvage is that it is discreet and effacing but present for a very long time, floating like a gentle veil behind the person wearing it."[22] Lemon, jasmine, and vetiver: The composition was simple and strict but revolutionary. Like Eau Fraîche, Eau Sauvage is a chypre—fittingly enough, this time the ladies started borrowing the perfume from their men, arguing that the gadroon on the bottle looked like the pleats of a couture dress and the cap seemed inspired by a thimble! In 2004, Bois d'Argent, created by Annick Ménardo, and Cologne Blanche and Eau Noire, both created by Francis Kurkdjian, all had the same effect: three fragrances from the Dior Homme fashion universe that appealed to women too.

"When you're looking for a name for a perfume that can appeal to an international audience, you always come up against oppositions: All the dictionaries in the world have been copyrighted, but this name wasn't. There must be a reason. Because no one dared to take it!"[23] Poison is ripe with subversion. Controlled arrogance. The traditional gray and white associated with Dior perfumes found itself replaced by amethyst and emerald green. Poison was the first ladies' perfume that did not echo the couturier's surname. Only the medallion inspired by the backs of the neo–Louis XVI chairs in the Avenue Montaigne flagship remains on the packaging, creating a unity with the other house fragrances—like a special beauty spot that the women in a given family all have in exactly the same place. I am a Dior perfume, it clearly states. But in this new context it is perceived differently, as an oval mirror in which we imagine a wicked queen inquiring: Who is the fairest of them all? Could it be someone else? The plump, round bottle suggests the form of an apple: the poison-ed fruit. Unlike Miss Dior, Poison started life as a name, around which the fragrance and the packaging were built. A daring perfume with a potent liturgy orchestrated to provoke temptation, the fragrance had high expectations to

> **Poison started life as a name, around which the fragrance and the packaging were built. A daring perfume with a potent liturgy orchestrated to provoke temptation.**

live up to: More than eight hundred proposals were made.[24] Poison wasn't going to whisper sweet nothings. Poison had to be risqué, a musky animal scent to set the pulse dizzily racing. But before reaching this sensual, bewitching end note, Poison glitters, flitters between coriander, pepper, and cinnamon accords. It weaves a mysterious web of spicy to fruity notes that create a tenacious sillage—ordinarily an oxymoron, the first evoking the persistence of the fragrance and the latter its diffuse presence. For there was never any question of Poison leaving darkness in its wake; the perfume is complex, enigmatic. It spurs an impulse for love and death in one breath. It celebrates a dangerous beauty, absolute femininity, the fantasy of Lucrezia Borgia assuaged, the Marquise de Brinvilliers brought to heel. "So what is Poison? It is nonconformism, flying in the face of convention; what we are recreating here is the Dior saga itself."[25]

Crystal chandeliers and halls of mirrors: After top model Carmen Kass's mythical bath of gold and Charlize Theron's striptease—"Gold is cold," she proclaimed at the time—the splendor of the Château de Versailles provided the setting for the latest J'adore opus in 2011. A pure concentrate of Dior aesthetics, this ninety-second film can be seen to encapsulate the saga of Dior perfumes. It clearly reaffirms the couturier's desire to associate his perfumes to his fashions: The setting is an Haute Couture runway show, reminiscent of the famous opening in 1947, when Miss Dior and the New Look redefined the canons of femininity. Close-up on Charlize Theron's towering heels as she runs through the

> " Diorling rings like darling.
> Then came Diorella, as fresh and spicy
> as a young woman sparkling in couture;
> Dior-Dior, a double-barreled Dior;
> and Dioressence, the utmost essence of Dior,
> consummate femininity. In J'adore too,
> no doubt, there is still a play on the name,
> in *adioration* of the master. "

Hall of Mirrors, sexy as hell in a chic black suit. She could be Belphegor, but really she is Diorella. Backstage, she meets the other models preparing for the show, greets Grace Kelly with a kiss, shares a look with Marlene Dietrich and Marilyn Monroe. These three actresses all wore Dior, but the marvels of technology enabled director Jean-Jacques Annaud to dress them in some of the couture house's very latest creations. Past and present tell the same story. Like this film, J'adore is quintessentially Dior. Calice Becker had only just turned thirty when she created this perfume. It is a youthful fragrance, as each of Dior's creations were likewise in their day. Bright as raw gold bullion, yet as meticulously crafted as a precious jewel. "Instead of creating a classic floral accord, I 'painted' each flower individually then brought them all together in a bouquet, to which I added a basket of lush fruit." Rose and lily of the valley are present, of course, but Christian Dior's two totemic blooms blend into a harmonious composition balanced between magnolia, violet, orchid, and carnation, a simple echo of the past. Christian Dior would have adored J'adore. He would have been transported back to his garden in Milly-la-Forêt from the very first note, an ode to his personal aesthetic and his obsession for novelty. A very twenty-first-century Dior.

Since that icy day back in February 1947, the saga of Dior perfumes reads like a great novel. Catherine, Christian's darling sister, the symbolic Miss and muse behind the limelight, kept her maiden name all life long, as though to ever remain the Miss Dior who inspired that first perfume. Christian died in 1957. Miss Dior, Diorama, Eau Fraîche, Diorissimo: Ten years brought only four fragrances, but each with its own radical approach. The result is an olfactory melody and a crystal-clear aesthetic. Christian Dior's legacy to the house he founded is a creative universe, a vision of perfumery intimately linked to his fashion. His successors have written new chapters in the story, drawing on his life and work for inspiration. Today François Demachy upholds the tradition as the house perfumer for Dior—a rare luxury. It is he who rewrites the main chapters in the House of Dior's history and dreams up those yet to come.

> 66 In Christian Dior's wildest dreams, he would have been able to create a fragrance for each of the looks in his couture show. 99

"The thing I remember most about the women in my childhood is their perfumes. They had a lasting fragrance, much more so than today, filling the air in the elevator long after the ladies had stepped out."[26] This confession from the couturier leaves no doubt as to his intentions as a perfumer. Christian Dior cloaked his memories in fragrance to bring the ladies from his childhood back to life. To materialize his olfactory memory.

**" I see myself as a perfumer
as much as a couturier. "**

Christian Dior

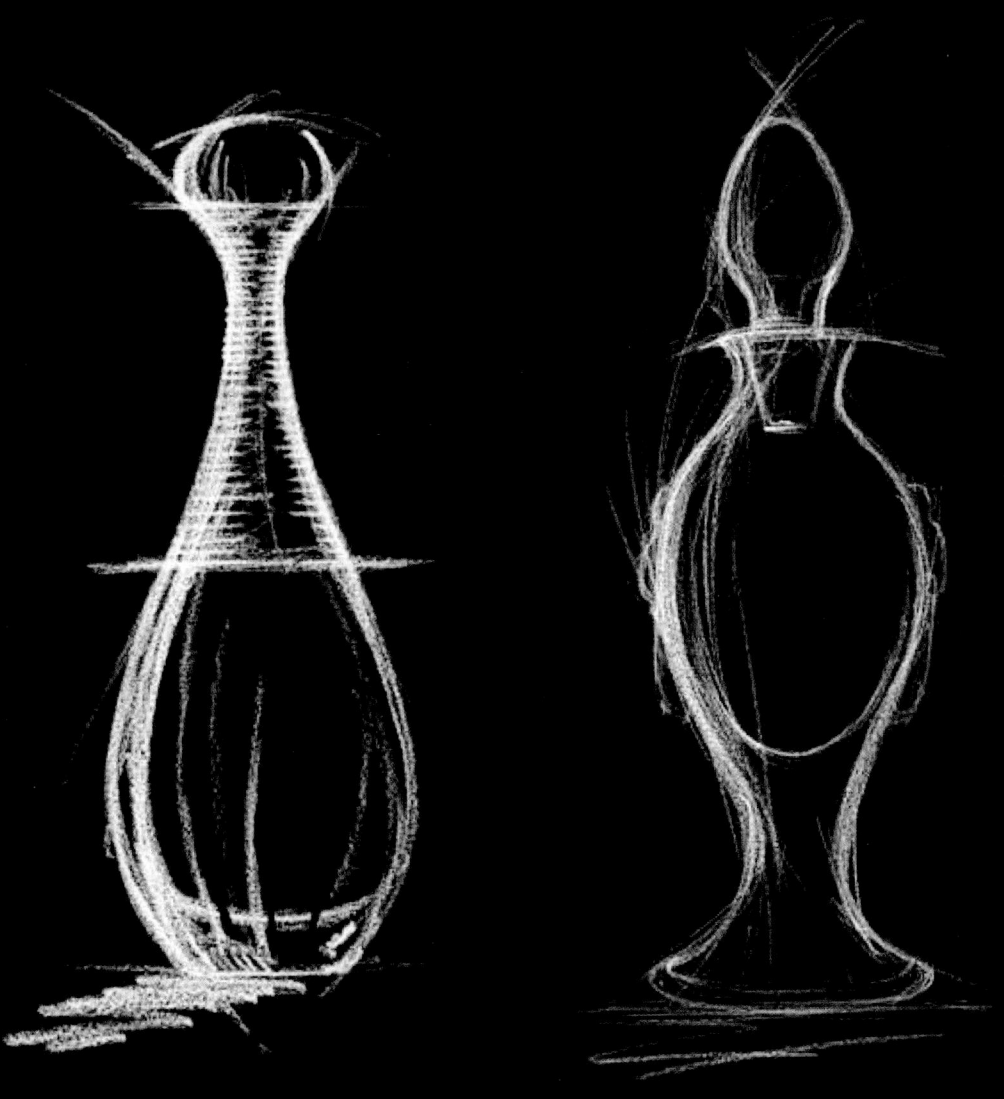

Christian Dior

présente

"Miss Dior"

Christian Dior

présente

"Miss Dior"

son premier parfum

exclusivement en son Hôtel, 30 Avenue Montaig:

à partir du 17 Decembre 1947.

Christian Dior

présente

"Miss Dior"

son premier par

Miss Dior

de Christian Dior

LE GRAND PARFUM DE NOTRE ÉPOQUE

après le sport...

...l'eau fraîche de

eau de cologne
fraîche
Christian
Dior

JUDE LAW IN A FILM BY GUY RITCHIE

DIOR HOMME

CHRISTIAN DIOR PARFUMS present DIOR HOMME

A FILM BY GUY RITCHIE STARRING JUDE LAW PICTURES BY PETER LINDBERGH MUSIC BY MUSE 'EXOGENESIS: SYMPHONY' (PART 1)

WWW.DIORHOMMEPARIS.COM

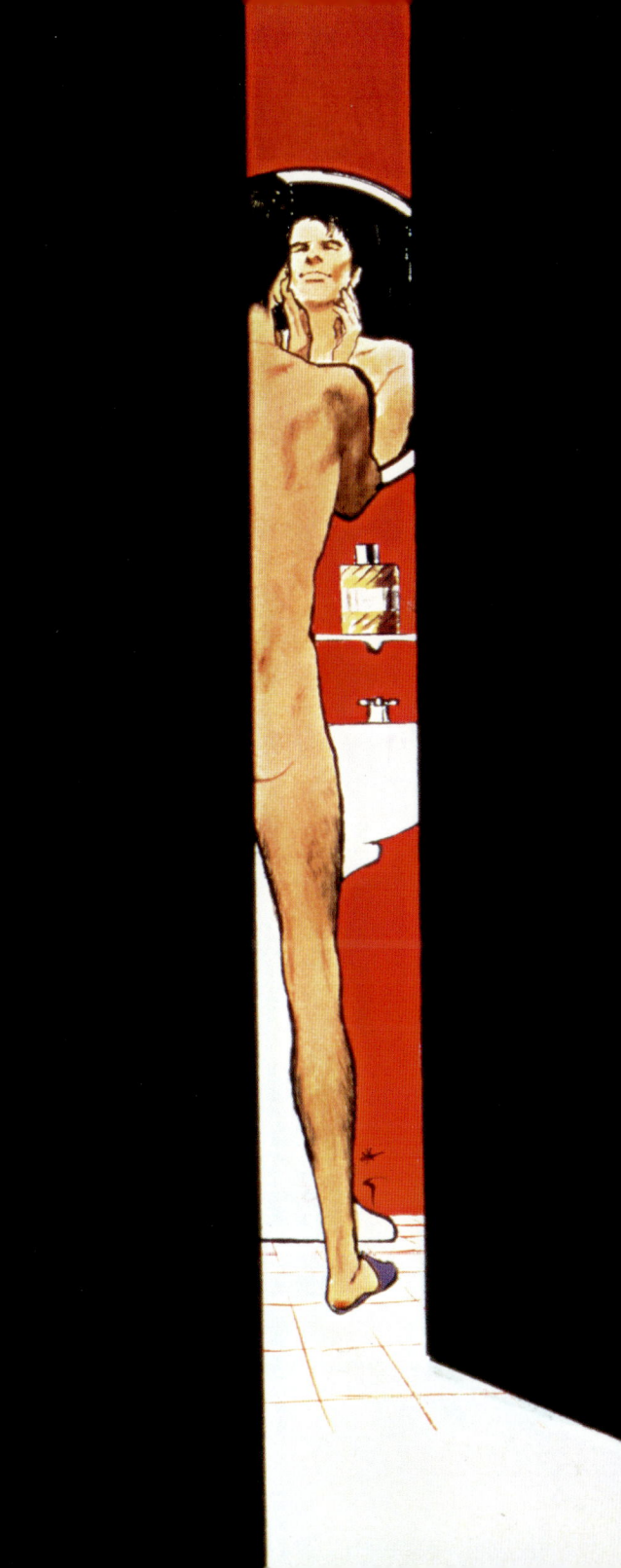

Notes

1. Christian Dior, interviewed circa 1950.
2. In order to be profitable, the perfume's life span must far exceed the seasonal nature of fashion.
3. Christian Dior wanted the most beautiful ingredients for his perfumes, the most noble raw materials of the highest quality. Today the House of Dior still uses flowers harvested exclusively for it, notably those from the Domaine de Manon in Grasse for jasmine and rose of May.
4. Edmond Roudnitska. Curriculum Vitae. In *Une Vie au service du parfum*, Thérèse Vian Éditions.
5. *Sous le signe du parfum: Edmond Roudnitska, Compositeur-Parfumeur*. Jocelyn and Jean-Paul Le Maquet. Marie-Christine Grasse. Jean-Claude Ellena. Éditions de l'Albaron, 1991.
6. Ever since Jicky, by Guerlain, in 1889—the first perfume to mix synthetic ingredients with natural essences—fragrant chemical compounds have revolutionized perfumery. Today they are present in every creation, and the perfume creator's possibilities are severely limited without them. Some can be quite harsh or brutal, however, so throughout the first half of the twentieth century perfumers softened them by using a high proportion of vanilla, fruity, or sweet notes. It is known as sweet or candy perfumery (see Edmond Roudnitska).
7. Edmond Roudnitska. Curriculum Vitae. In *Une Vie au service du parfum*, Thérèse Vian Éditions.
8. Spring-Summer 1950.
9. A perfume trilogy created by the house perfumer-creator, François Demachy: Escale à Portofino in 2008, Escale à Pondichéry in 2009 and Escale aux Marquises in 2010.
10. Christian Dior, lecture given for the French Civilization course at the Sorbonne University in Paris on August 3, 1955.
11. Spring-Summer 1955. There were three other outfits named Rosée in Christian Dior's lifetime: Fall-Winter 1947, Spring-Summer 1956, and Spring-Summer 1957.
12. Spring-Summer 1954; Fall-Winter 1952.
13. Fall-Winter 1953.
14. Spring-Summer 1949; Fall-Winter 1950; Fall-Winter 1953 and 1957; Fall-Winter 1956.
15. Translator's note: In order of mention, the English flower names are: acacia, daisy, petunia, reseda, forget-me-not, lily, iris, poppy, dahlia, hydrangea, lupine, carnation, colza, buttercup, angelica, and scabious.
16. Spring-Summer 1953.
17. Spring-Summer 1952.
18. Spring-Summer 1951; Spring-Summer 1952; Spring-Summer 1953.
19. Spring-Summer 1948; Spring-Summer 1949; Fall-Winter 1947.
20. Spring-Summer 1949; Spring-Summer 1951.
21. Fall-Winter 1950 and 1952.
22. *Sous le signe du parfum: Edmond Roudnitska, Compositeur-Parfumeur*. Le Maquet et al.
23. Speech given in Monte Carlo by Maurice Roger, then president of Parfums Christian Dior, on June 17, 1985, for the launch of Poison.
24. In the 1980s, the world of perfumery entered a period of highly competitive transformation. To stand out, the launch of Poison enjoyed a huge budget for its day. Advertising campaign, commercial directed by Claude Chabrol, a grand ball held for the official launch at the Château Vaux-le-Vicomte in France—a global communications budget estimated at $40 million.
25. Speech by Maurice Roger in Monte Carlo.
26. Christian Dior, *Je suis couturier*. Interviewed by Alice Chavane and Elie Rabourdin. Éditions du Conquistador (1951, out of print).

Chronology

1947:	Introduction of Miss Dior at the New Look couture show, February 12.
1949:	Launch of Diorama, the first perfume created by Edmond Roudnitska.
1955:	Launch of L'Eau Fraîche, the first unisex eau de cologne.
1956:	Launch of Diorissimo, Dior's good luck perfume.
1963:	Launch of Diorling.
1966:	Launch of L'Eau Sauvage for men with a complete line of products, a first in perfumery.
1972:	For the launch of Diorella, René Gruau draws the first Dior woman to wear pants in an advertisement.
1979:	Dioresscence was first introduced in 1973 as a bath line, then as a perfume.
1980:	Launch of Jules, the first sport fragrance by Christian Dior Perfumes.
1985:	Launch of Poison at the Vaux-le-Vicomte château, September 17.
1988:	Launch of Fahrenheit.
1998:	Launch of Hypnotic Poison.
1999:	Launch of J'adore.
2002:	Launch of Dior Addict.
2005:	Launch of Dior Homme.
2008:	Launch of Escale à Portofino.
2011:	La Collection Privée Christian Dior.

Christian Dior at 30 Avenue Montaigne, circa 1955. The couturier himself saw to the flower arrangements and encouraged his staff to spritz the salons with Dior perfumes. Photo © 2011 Association Willy Maywald/Artists Rights Society (ARS), New York/ADAGP, Paris

Dior

PERFUME

Christian Dior in his garden at Milly-la-Forêt, circa 1953. A great connoisseur of flowers and their fragrances, Dior designed the gardens at his houses at Milly-la-Forêt and Montauroux himself. Photo © André Ostier. **Flowers from the garden at villa Les Rhumbs in Granville, Dior's childhood home.** Christian Dior acquired a passion for roses very early in life, inspired by their colors, shapes, and delicate scent. Photo © 2008 Musée Christian Dior.

The gardens at Versailles Palace and the style of the court of the Sun King inspired Christian Dior's fragrance creations. Photo © Jose Fuste Raga/Corbis. **Illustration by René Gruau for Miss Dior, 1961.** From 1947, Gruau celebrated his friend Christian Dior's "flower women," and his illustrations expressed the intangibility of perfume. Photo © SARL René Gruau/www.renegruau.com.

Christian Dior, couturier-perfumer. The evolution of the En Huit (Figure 8) line of 1947 to the amphora design of the original Miss Dior flacon to today's J'adore bottle. Christian Dior always believed that "Perfume is the finishing touch to a dress." Photo © 2010 Christian Dior Perfumes.

J'adore by Jean-Baptiste Mondino. The first campaign for J'adore, featuring model Carmen Kass, paid homage to the radiant power of absolute femininity. Photo: Jean-Baptiste Mondino © Christian Dior Perfumes.

J'adore by Patrick Demarchelier. The face of Dior since 2004, Charlize Theron has revealed the personality of the fragrance through the lenses of the greatest photographers. Photo: Patrick Demarchelier © Christian Dior Perfumes. **J'adore by Jean-Jacques Annaud.** Filmed in the Hall of Mirrors at Versailles, this campaign for J'adore was an ode to femininity. Photo © 2011 Christian Dior Perfumes.

Applying the gold collar to the J'adore bottle. Faithful to its heritage of craftsmanship, Dior continues to refine the art of perfumery by releasing special editions, featuring touches such as frosted and hand-cut crystal, gilding, and engraving of the star motif, one of Christian Dior's lucky charms. Photo: Philippe Schlienger © 1999 Christian Dior Perfumes. **J'adore l'Absolue.** From eau de toilette to more concentrated versions, Dior uses the highest quality ingredients. Photo © 2010 Christian Dior Perfumes.

The Bar suit, 1947. The most famous ensemble from the first Christian Dior Haute Couture collection in February 1947, the Bar suit represented the new, more architectural standard of classic Parisian elegance. Photo © 2011 Association Willy Maywald/Artists Rights Society (ARS), New York/ADAGP, Paris. **New Look 1947**, one of the fragrances in La Collection Privée, which marries couture and perfumery traditions to produce modern expressions of the master's vision. Photo © 2011 Christian Dior Perfumes.

Invitation to the launch of Miss Dior, 1947. As with his Haute Couture collections, Dior celebrated the launch of his first fragrance by inviting clients and journalists to 30 Avenue Montaigne. With Miss Dior, he wanted to create "a perfume with the fragrance of love." Photo © Christian Dior Perfumes. **The original Baccarat crystal Miss Dior amphora bottle, 1951**, with opalescent crystal overlaid on clear crystal, the subtle play of materials expressing the refinement of Dior Haute Couture. Photo: Philippe Schlienger © Christian Dior Perfumes.

Miss Dior dress from the Spring-Summer 1949 Haute Couture collection. The allover floral embroidery of the Miss Dior cocktail dress calls to mind the flowers used in the perfume, the dress becoming an expression of the fragrance. Photo © Laziz Hamani. **Natalie Portman.** The face of Miss Dior, Natalie Portman embodies the romantic and saucy young Dior woman from yesterday to today. Photo: Tim Walker © 2010 Christian Dior Perfumes.

Miss Dior by René Gruau, 1949. Christian Dior and Gruau shared a love of classicism. The pearl-white swan, symbol of youth in the 18th century, was used by Gruau for the first Miss Dior advertisement. Photo © SARL René Gruau/www.renegruau.com. **Miss Dior bottle, 1950.** After the amphora, Christian Dior designed a more architectural version for Miss Dior, incorporating the bow and houndstooth pattern. Photo © Christian Dior Perfumes.

The original Baccarat crystal flacon for Diorissimo, designed by Christian Dior, 1956. This edition was topped with a floral bouquet stopper in fine gold, representing the flowers in the perfume. Photo © Christian Dior Perfumes. **Brigitte Bardot receiving Diorissimo at 30 Avenue Montaigne, 1960.** Undeniable icon of the 1960s, Brigitte Bardot was invited to discover the single-floral Diorissimo fragrance by Edmond Roudnitska, an expression of lily of the valley, Christian Dior's favorite flower. Photo © Christian Dior Perfumes.

Mitzah Bricard. Leopard-print ensemble from the Fall-Winter 2009 Haute Couture collection, in homage to Mitzah Bricard, Christian Dior's muse and ally; he thought of her as the ambassador of refinement. Photo: Thibaut de Saint-Chamas. **Mitzah, one of the fragrances in La Collection Privée.** In 2010, François Demachy created a sensual oriental perfume for Dior christened Mitzah, a fragrance recalling the feline and spiritual femininity of Mitzah Bricard. Photo © Laziz Hamani.

Diorama by René Gruau, 1961. A Venetian Carnival disguise was chosen to represent Diorama. René Gruau paid homage to the grand society balls so dear to Christian Dior in the 1950s. Photo © SARL René Gruau/www.renegruau.com. **Diorama Obelisk flacon, 1955.** Created in clear Baccarat crystal, this limited edition recalls the obelisk of the Place de la Concorde and Christian Dior's love of Paris. Photo: Philippe Schlienger © Christian Dior Perfumes.

Eau Fraîche by René Gruau, 1955. The illustrator chose a sporty ambience for the first cologne by Christian Dior Perfumes. Photo © SARL René Gruau/www.renegruau.com. **Eau de Cologne Fraîche, 1955.** Early on, Christian Dior launched travel editions for his international clientele. Flacons in silvertone metal were designed for Eau Fraîche to better preserve the fragrance. Photo: Philippe Schlienger © Christian Dior Perfumes.

Fine ingredients. The same way the best fabrics are chosen for Haute Couture, the fragrance components are selected according to the highest standards of quality and provenance. Photo © 2010 Christian Dior Perfumes. **The 18th century.** In this 1955 photograph of the Christian Dior Parfums boutique, the grand decorative motifs of the 18th century can be seen: Trianon gray, the Fontange bow, and sunray pleats all serve to showcase the Dior fragrances and cosmetics. Photo © Christian Dior Perfumes.

Princess Grace of Monaco at the opening of the Baby Dior boutique in 1967. The first collection designed for children, Baby Dior offered a range of products, including an eau de cologne. Photo: Courtesy Christian Dior Archives. **Chest of Christian Dior Perfumes offered to Princess Grace of Monaco in 1961.** This 19th-century lacquered box contained a luxury edition of Diorissimo perfume and an assortment of 14 Dior lipsticks. Photo © Philippe Schlienger.

Eau Sauvage by Gruau, 1978. René Gruau could depict everyday situations with humor and a wink of impertinence. The nude gentleman here holds a flacon of Eau Sauvage in place of a glass of whiskey. Photo © SARL René Gruau/www.renegruau.com. **Eau Sauvage by Dominique Issermann.** This emblematic visual from 1987 is the first photograph for an Eau Sauvage campaign after the ones illustrated by Gruau. "The man at the barre" offered a new virile and mysterious image for Eau Sauvage. Photo © Dominique Issermann.

Eau Sauvage by Jean-Marie Périer, 1966. Classic and timeless, Eau Sauvage is the fragrance of great modern legends, such as Alain Delon, who represents the eternal masculine. Photo © Jean-Marie Périer. **Eau Sauvage flacon, 1966.** This bottle, created by Pierre Carnin, is a modern blend of feminine and masculine design styles. Photo © Christian Dior Perfumes.

Poison by Tyen, 1985. Thanks to an extensive global campaign by Tyen and Claude Chabrol, Poison became a worldwide phenomenon that led to new versions such as Hypnotic Poison in 1998 and Pure Poison in 2006. Photos: Tyen © Christian Dior Perfumes.

Poison by Tyen. In 1985, Poison wrote a new page in the history of Christian Dior, becoming the first in a new generation of perfumes inspired by an evocative name and the extreme possibilities of the world of fragrance. Photo: Tyen © Christian Dior Perfumes. **Poison bottle, 1985.** The flacon's form calls to mind a fruit or a volcano, two strong ideas embodied in the power of the perfume's oriental essences. Photo © Christian Dior Perfumes.

Milla Jovovich for Hypnotic Poison, 1998. Directed by Jean-Baptiste Mondino, the advertisement video for Hypnotic Poison featured a fascinating and possibly even dangerous woman, the ideal role for Milla Jovovich, who was first showcased by Luc Besson in 1997 in *The Fifth Element*. Photo © Jean-Baptiste Mondino. **Mélanie Laurent for Hypnotic Poison, 2011.** Photo © Christian Dior Perfumes.

Dior Addict flacon, 2002. Photo © Christian Dior Perfumes. **Dior Addict by Nick Knight, 2002.** Dior Addict explores an unbridled sexiness, magnificently illustrated by the extreme visuals of Nick Knight. The use of avant-garde fashion photography is an electrifying step forward in the story of Christian Dior Perfumes. Photo © Nick Knight.

Fahrenheit by Ridley Scott. Upon its launch in 1988, Fahrenheit was a terrific success. The rich fragrance conjures images of wide-open spaces. Photo: Knut Bry © Christian Dior Perfumes. **The Fahrenheit bottle** is innovative, with its gradated sunset hues and profile reminiscent of a lighthouse. Photo: Laziz Hamani © 2010 Christian Dior Perfumes.

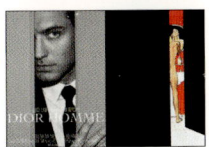

Still from an advertising video directed by Guy Ritchie for the Dior Homme campaign starring Jude Law, 2011. Photo: Peter Lindbergh © Christian Dior Perfumes. **René Gruau for Eau Sauvage, 1978.** Gruau helped define the image of modern masculinity by showing a man in the intimacy of the bathroom, an audaciously original setting. Photo © SARL René Gruau/www.renegruau.com.

Dior Homme Intense, created in 2005. Dior Homme represents a strong and timeless masculinity, embodied by Jude Law since 2008. Photos © 2011 Christian Dior Perfumes.

The Miss Dior packaging, 1950. Since 1947, Christian Dior applied his Haute Couture motifs to his perfume creations, like the houndstooth pattern, calligraphic script, and variations on the name "Dior," embodying the universe he created at 30 Avenue Montaigne and disseminating it around the world. Photo © Christian Dior Perfumes.

Acknowledgments

The publisher wishes to thank the Maison Dior for its help in the publication of this book.

Thanks also to: Denise Raab Jacobs; Thomas Michael Gunther, André Ostier; Sylvie Nissen, SARL René Gruau; Laziz Hamani; Alexandra Kadlec, Artists Rights Society; Anne Porto, Corbis.